VERTEBRATE MEMORY
Characteristics and Origin

VERTEBRATE MEMORY
Characteristics and Origin

I. S. Beritashvili
(J. S. Beritoff)

Institute of Physiology
Georgian Academy of Sciences
Tbilisi, USSR

Translated by John S. Barlow

Department of Neurology
Massachusetts General Hospital
and
Harvard Medical School
Boston, Massachusetts

With an Introduction by the Translation Editor
W. T. Liberson

Veteran's Administration Hospital
Miami, Florida

ℚ PLENUM PRESS • NEW YORK–LONDON • 1971

The original Russian text, published by Metsniereba Press in Tbilisi in 1968, has been extensively revised and corrected by the author for the present edition, which is published under an agreement with Mezhdunarodnaya Kniga, the Soviet book export agency.

И. С. БЕРИТАШВИЛИ

ПАМЯТЬ ПОЗВОНОЧНЫХ ЖИВОТНЫХ
ЕЁ ХАРАКТЕРИСТИКА И ПРОИСХОЖДЕНИЕ

PAMYAT' POZVONOCHNYKH ZHIVOTNYKH
EE KHARAKTERISTIKA I PROISKHOZHDENIE

Library of Congress Catalog Card Number 74-157930
SBN 306-30524-0

Introduction to the English Edition

Five years ago, I introduced to the English speaking scientific community the work of Professor Beritashvili by translating and editing his major monograph *Neural Mechanisms of Higher Vertebrate Behavior*, which appeared in Russian in 1961.[1] Of advanced age (over 80) and preeminent as dean of Soviet neurophysiology, he was nevertheless virtually unknown in this country at that time, except to a select circle of neurophysiologists who had had occasion to meet him at international meetings since before the first World War. Prior to the Soviet publication of the present monograph in 1968, Professor Beritashvili had published ten books and yet another has appeared since. Besides being a prolific author, he has been the editor of a large number of works documenting many yearly neurophysiological conferences held in his native Georgia.

Professor Beritashvili, whose contributions to neurophysiology started in 1911, has been working in all fields of this science, from nerve fibers and the spinal cord to the highest levels of brain activity. However, his major contribution has been a demonstration of the universality of learning following a single presentation of an object vitally important to an animal, whether it be a food object or a nociceptive agent. He postulates that following a single such presentation, an "image" of this object may be formed in the brain of an animal, and, thereafter, behavior proceeds as if the animal actually saw the object. Beritashvili showed that such "image-driven" behavior has a strong spatial component, i.e., the image is projected into a definite point in

---

[1] Beritashvili, I. S. (Beritoff, J. S.) (1965). *Neural Mechanisms of Higher Vertebrate Behavior*, W. T. Liberson (ed.). [Transl. from Russian] Little, Brown, and Company, Boston, p. 384.

space. This observation led Beritashvili to devote years of his scientific work to the problems of spatial perception and orientation. Thus, Beritashvili and his numerous associates maintain that, in addition to Pavlovian learning by conditioning involving repetition of association, there is image-driven behavior which does not necessitate such repetition. They showed that, by applying different experimental procedures, one may reveal that these two different modes of learning are supported by different functional processes and anatomical structures. For example, an animal subjected to concussion may cease to exhibit image-driven behavior, but not elementary conditioned reflexes. A decorticated animal may be conditioned by repeated associations but is unable after a single presentation of the event to remember it, and, therefore, to form an image.

The present monograph summarizes the research carried out in his laboratory since the preparation of his earlier translated monograph mentioned above. He reviews in the present book pertinent literature and presents challenging blueprints of the organization of structures supporting higher brain activities. In this monograph, Beritashvili asks and attempts to answer different questions from those discussed in his previous book. If learning is the base of memory, how does memory differ when it is established on image formation following a single association from that which is rooted in conditioning processes requiring many associations? How do these memories differ when the animal deals with a rewarding experience or with a frustrating one? Which are the structures and functions underlying each of these memories? How are these processes related to the modern concept of short-term and long-term memories, the latter allegedly rooted in the processes of formation of highly specialized active proteins? Most importantly, how do these two kinds of memories express themselves in phylogeny from fish to man and in ontogeny during postembryonic development? The reader is then taken through a succession of experiments which reveal to him a monumental body of data. The following are but a few examples: To the notion of the primary role allegedly played by the hippocampus in memory function, Beritashvili opposes the priority of the proreal gyrus in dogs and prefrontal cortex in baboons, at least as far as image memory is concerned. In lower animals conditioned memory does not depend on the cortex, and in fish the cerebellum is one of the structures which support conditioning. The study of a short-term or long-term image, conditioned, and emotional memory in phylogeny constitute one of the most fascinating chapters of this monograph. The author shows how short-term memory evolves in fish, where it is measured in seconds, in reptiles, where it is measured in minutes, and in mammals, where it is measured in hours. Long-term image memory appears first in birds and lasts for months in baboons after a single presentation of the object to be remembered. Long-term image memory depends on many factors, among them novelty, which considerably prolongs the persistence of memory. It may last for more than a month even in dogs. Beritashvili shows the similarity, if not the identity, of delayed reactions during conditioned and image memory. Here he joins forces with many Western investigators who, like Pribram, have studied the anatomical basis for such reactions.[2]

Finally, he shows that ontogeny recapitulates phylogeny as far as image memory is concerned. It is truly amazing how much data this investigator has accumulated during the seven years separating these two monographs. He and his associates continue to accumulate new data and the present English edition incorporates results of research which will appear in the second Russian edition.

Granted, some of the postulates will have to be readjusted in the course of future experimentation; also, the difference between the image memory of normal and decorticated animals is sometimes quantitative rather than absolute. However, the major thesis will undoubtedly remain, and the concluding chapters of this work, related to a phylogenetic and postembryonic development of image, short-term, long-term, emotional, and conditioned memories as well as of other aspects of learning and adaptive psychophysiological behavior in animals, will have to be considered another milestone in physiological literature.

As a matter of fact, one is at times disappointed to find that the author does not extend his speculations further. Beritashvili succeeded in rehabilitating the term "image" to a place of respectability, after Pavlovians had banned it from animal psychophysiology. In the process of restoring this concept, Beritashvili suffered indignities from the Stalinist scientific bureaucracy. Pavlov ignored this term as a matter of scientific tactics and strategy, rather than owing to a real conviction. No one who has access to the company of pets will deny their ability to project into a hidden environment the anticipation of a desirable object that they saw there only once. Personally, I prefer the term "phantom" (such as the phantoms of amputees) to "image," so that a visual perception is not literally implied. What "image" means is an anticipation, an expectancy of an event to come, and no one will deny that these anticipatory processes are the essence of brain activity. To be able to contain all "phantoms" of the animal world within the brain and to make them interact, whether they be stirred from within or prompted from without, is the very meaning of higher processes of brain activity. Pavlov rebelled against considering such concepts because he did not have at his disposal, at that time, experimental methods able to deal with them objectively. With the advent of modern electrophysiology, some of these processes may be

---

[2] Pribram, K. H., (1950). *J. Neurophysiol.* **13**: 373–382.

Introduction to the English Edition

translated into electrical events. In fact, recording of anticipatory spikes (Liberson and Ellen)[3] and expectancy waves (Walter)[4] offers new opportunities in this direction. In particular, the introduction by John and Killam,[5] of the methodology of "trace rhythms" and our demonstration of their disappearance after many repetitions of association may in fact be related to the emergence of phantoms during short-term memory.

Most importantly, from this viewpoint, the difference between the memory resulting from a single presentation of an object and the memory related to the object's repeated perception may be only the difference in *kind of repetition*. A single presentation of an object may be followed by multiple reproductions of its "phantoms" in the brain of a motivated animal, and thus, in the final analysis in *both* cases, memory depends on repetition of perceptions reinforced by either an unconditioned stimulus or its phantom.

In the present monograph, Professor Beritashvili provides us with a vivid description of what may go on in the brain of the animal. During the time preceding the release of a baboon from its cage, after a single presentation of food, which was then hidden behind a screen, the animal was" shaking the cage, attempting to open the door, crying out continually. . . ." How many times was the food "phantom" reproduced in the brain of this animal during the period of waiting, which lasted as long as an hour? During this time, the animal was probably successful in repeatedly reproducing the memory of food. Then, the difference of the "image memory" from "conditioned memory" is not only the number of repetitions, but rather the ability of the brain to repeatedly reproduce the phantoms of the outside world, thus providing a mechanism for the regeneration of percepts from within. This appears to be the true meaning of the phylogenetic development of the brain.

It is because of these fascinating speculations which are nourished by Beritashvili's contribution that I accepted his request to edit and translate his book and two other papers, despite many other commitments. It was after my work had started that I had the good fortune to learn that Dr. John S. Barlow had offered his services to Professor Beritashvili for the translation of the same monograph. Dr. Barlow was the ideal person to undertake this task and bring it to rapid fruition. He is a neurophysiologist of repute, a linguist, and an experienced translator of scientific publications, possessing intimate knowledge of the subject matter. I was grateful to him for this

[3] Liberson, W. T. and Ellen, P., (1960). Conditioning of the driven brain wave rhythm in the cortex and the hippocampus of the rat. In *Recent Advances in Biological Psychiatry*, Grune and Stratton, Inc., pp. 158–171.

[4] Walter, W. G., (1964). Slow potential waves in the human brain associated with expectancy, attenuation, and decision. *Arch. Psychiat. Nervenkr.* **206**: 309–322.

[5] John, E. R. and Killam, K., (1959). *In* Mary A. B. Brazier (ed.) *The Central Nervous System and Behavior*, Josiah Macy, Jr. Foundation, New York, p. 33.

offer and was happy to be of help to him, when, not being a native Russian, he was challenged by an idiom or a biological term which was difficult for him to identify. He has succeeded in retaining in many instances the flavor of Russian sentence construction and often I have hesitated to break this charm.

W. T. LIBERSON

Author's Preface

We began the study of memory in animals in the Department of Human and Animal Physiology of Tbilisi University in the beginning of the 1930's. At that time we initiated studies of both conditioned-reflex feeding behavior as well as image behavior, i.e., according to the image of location of food. All of these forms of feeding behavior constitute manifestations of memory, since they are based on the retention of structural and biochemical consequences of those processes in the cerebral cortex which arise at the time of a single or repeated perception of the food object and its location.

In 1933, the Institute of Experimental Biology was founded on the grounds of the Department of Physiology at Tbilisi University. Then, in 1935 the Institute of Physiology was established, which in 1941 became a part of the Academy of Sciences of the Georgian Soviet Socialist Republic. The study of these forms of behavior also became the principal object of investigation in these institutes. In 1933 and 1934, 10 articles on individually-acquired feeding behavior were published in the *Physiological Journal of the USSR*. In these papers, a set of factors characterizing psychoneural memory in relation to feeding behavior was defined: the origin of the image of the location of food, its retention, and its reproduction after some time, either on the order of minutes, hours, or days after a single perception of the food object.

This psychoneural image memory was initially studied in dogs, but shortly other vertebrates also became the objects of investigation—rabbits, cats, chickens, pigeons, and also man, including normal children and microcephalics. All of this work thus constituted an extensive comparative investigation of psychoneural memory.

On the basis of analysis of the factual material that had been accumulated, we then established a series of characteristics of image psychoneural activity, relevant both to animals and to man. This part of our study was summarized in 1947 in the book, *On the Basic Forms of Neural and Psychoneural Activity*.

Then, in the 1940's and 1950's, we carried out a multifaceted study of spatial orientation in the environment, one of the higher forms of psychic activity of vertebrates and man. In the study of spatial orientation, which is based entirely on psychic memory, we come even closer to the study of the latter. The roles of visual, auditory, vestibular, olfactory, and proprioceptive receptors, and the dependence of memory on them for orientation in space were investigated, along with the roles of different regions of the cortex and other parts of the brain in these manifestations of memory. The results of this investigation were summarized in 1959 in the book, *On Neural Mechanisms of Spatial Orientation in Higher Vertebrates*.

In the last ten years we have set ourselves the goal of a multifaceted study of the origin of image memory in different representatives of the vertebrate series, from fish to monkeys inclusively.

We first established the characteristic features of image memory for visual, auditory, vestibular, gustatory, and olfactory perception, individually, of a food object, as well as for complex perception of it, i.e., in which more than one sensory modality participates. We also studied the origin of emotional and conditioned-reflex memory in these animals. We attempted to clarify the manner in which various parts of the archipaleocortex (i.e., the old cortex) and the neocortex (i.e., the new cortex), and subcortical structures participate in these phenomena of memory, and the neurophysiological, neurohistological, and neurochemical bases for each of these forms of memory. We were also able to obtain a great deal of information on the manner in which characteristic features of memory varied with different functional states of the organism.

The present book basically contains the results of this aspect of the study of memory. On the other hand, we are only at the initial stages of studies of the neurobiochemical and neurostructural bases of memory, as is also the case in many other neurophysiological and psychological laboratories of the world in which memory is being studied.

Many older and younger scientific colleagues in the Department of Physiology at the Tbilisi State University and at the Institute of Physiology have collaborated in this investigation of memory (the names of all of whom will be given in the text). Thus, their role in the study of memory will be evident. Here I shall only mention, first of all, those who played a leading role in the initial study of individually-acquired behavior: A. N. Bregadze, N. N. Dzidzishvili, and then those who played a similar role later: I. M. Aivazashvili, A. N. Bakuradze, P. A. Kometiani, M. R. Kuparadze, A. L. Mikeladze, T. N. Oniani, Ts. A. Ordzhonikidze, and A. I. Roitbak.

Contents

Vertebrate Memory

PRELIMINARY INFORMATION CONCERNING MEMORY

In higher vertebrates (birds and mammals) memory is manifested as the recall both of a single occasion of the animal's subjective experience of perception of the external world, as well as the single instance of adaptation to a specific change in the environment. This type of psychical activity plays an important role in the individual behavior of the animal. It is based on the retention of images of the perceived external world and on their reproduction at the time of the repetition of the effect of the perceived object or of a part of it, or on the reappearance of the surroundings of the object when it was perceived. In this process, not only the subjective reflection of the given object and its location is reproduced, but also an external response which ensued on the original occasion can arise. Thus by reproduction of the image of any given object of vital importance, the animal responds as though it had perceived the corresponding object itself. For example, as is well known, domesticated animals (cats, dogs, chickens, pigeons) remember the appearance, the amount, and type of food, and its location in the environment. They also remember the appearance, dwelling, and other signs of enemies after a single adverse encounter. Outwardly, image memory appears after perception of an object of vital importance, so that the animal can react appropriately, not only immediately after the perception, but after an appreciable time measured in minutes, hours, days, etc. In the case of perception of food, the animal approaches the place of feeding; if danger is perceived, it avoids this location or runs away from it (Beritashvili, 1939).

Memory also appears as a reproduction of conditioned reflex movement

1

and secretory responses, or learned, habitual movements a long time after its formation. When a particular indifferent stimulus becomes a conditional one, evoking feeding behavior as a result of multiple reinforcement during the act of feeding, then the stimulus evokes the corresponding behavior after days or months following the last reinforcement with feeding. Finally, memory is apparent in the genesis of emotional experience—fear, rage, pleasant or unpleasant sensations, conditions of anxiety, etc., under the influence of indifferent objects that are accompanied by the experience of these emotions. For example, let us assume that, at the time of eating from a feeder standing in a particular location in a room, the animal receives an electric shock. This painful stimulus evokes intense fear of the particular feeder and its surroundings; the animal jumps aside and runs away. Cats or dogs will exhibit such fear before this feeder upon being led to it, whether the next day, or after many days.

Together with our co-workers, we have studied these phenomena of memory for more than 30 years, and considered them earlier than many other neurophysiologists and psychologists. We will not give here a detailed historical survey of earlier work by other investigators, but shall only mention a few authors for support or illustration of our theoretical views.

All authors who have studied memory in animals have delineated two aspects or two forms of memory. Konorski (1959), one of the most active contemporary investigators of memory in animals, characterizes them in the following way. In the first form, there is a stable or permanent form of memory which is based on a stable micromorphological plastic change in central connections. The second form is ascribed to circulation of excitation in closed neural circuits which can persist for some time. The latter form is termed recent, immediate, or dynamic memory. Hebb (1961) has characterized these two forms of memory in approximately the same way.

We find this classification of memory insufficient, for it is not in accord with the results of our own studies.

METHODS OF STUDY OF MEMORY

We used different methods for the study of memory, the particular method depending on the particular task. Our work entailed (1) visual perception of objects and the retention of their images; (2) auditory perception and the retention of an auditory image—the direction of the sound and its source; (3) vestibular perception and the retention of the image of the path traversed; (4) complex perception of an object by means of several sensory organs: vision, olfaction, taste, and the vestibular perception; (5) emotional stimuli in the form of fear; and finally (6) conditioned reflex behavior following the perception of a conditional signal.

Visual Perception. In a large experimental room (6 × 10 m) large or small screens stood at a distance of 2 to 8 m from a screened cage where the animal was located. The animal could not see all of them at the same time because of the way the screens were placed (Fig. 1). Usually, we showed

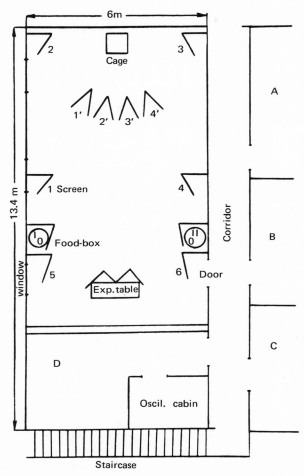

Fig. 1. Experimental arrangement for study of memory by the method of free movement. At the rear wall of the large experimental room stands the cage which is opened and closed automatically. The experimenter's table is in front of the cage at a distance of 6 m, and is enclosed by high screens with slits through which observations on the behavior of the animal are carried out. Small screens in different locations in the experimental room are denoted by 1, 2, 3, 4, 5, and 6, behind which the food is placed. The small screens denoted by 1', 2', 3', and 4', which are in a single visual field at a distance of 1½ m from the cage, are also used in some experiments. When other experiments are carried out involving the showing or eating of food, the latter screens are removed. I and II are feeders which automatically open and close, from which the animal feeds during the formation of conditioned feeding behavior. In the study of long-term memory, the animal is first led across the corridor into one of the rooms opposite the experimental room (A, B, C, or D), and is then brought to a particular feeding location.

a dish with food at a distance of $1\frac{1}{2}$ to 2 m within sight of the animal, then took it away and put it down behind one of the screens so that the animal could see the procedure. After a short time, we released the animal from the cage. If it went immediately and directly to the location of the food, we assumed that the feeding behavior was carried out on the basis of an image of this location. After it had eaten, we returned the animal to the cage. Subsequently, over the course of several minutes, there were three more releases from the cage without reinforcement; the animal initially went to the same place where it had fed; then it did not go there or did not even go out of the cage. Only after this did we carry out the next trial, in which food was brought to another location.

The screens behind which the food was placed were not always in the same places; they were transferred from place to place, or a new screen was set down in a new place in the room, and the food that had been shown was set down behind them. In this way we avoided conditioning the animals to a particular location for feeding.

By releasing the animal after different intervals of time, we determined not only the duration of retention in memory of the image of food, but also the image of the visually perceived location of food and the direction to the latter.

In some instances, we carried food to the animal, so that it could sense the odor and attempt to grasp and feel the food; only then was the latter taken away and set down behind the screen.

Auditory Perception. The animal wore a light-tight mask on its head, to which it had become accustomed. In a particular location in the experimental room, the food basin was struck against the floor, so that the noise from the basin constituted a natural conditional feeding signal. Sometimes this place was denoted on the floor by means of a circle. The animal had to determine the place of food from perception of the direction of the source of the noise. When this noise occurred, the animal went directly to the source of the noise. We then determined for how long a time the animal could retain the image of the direction and location of the source of the sound distinctively enough to go directly to this location.

In certain cases, we did not place the mask on the animal but covered the cage with screens and struck the basin somewhere in the room, either in an open space, or behind some obstacle. After varying intervals of time, the cage was opened, and the animal, going around the obstacle, went to the source of the noise. We thus established the maximum interval after which the animal would not go directly to the source of the sound.

Vestibular Perception of a Path. The animal, trained with the mask, i.e., with eyes covered, was seated in the cage and was carried to various places in the experimental room. There the animal was let out of the cage and placed at the basin of food, allowed to scent it, then was led back to the cage and put back in the original location. Wearing the mask, the animal was then released from the cage, and the time was determined within which it could still proceed directly to the place of food.

Complex Perception of the Location of Food. We led the animal out of the cage to one of the screens, allowed it to smell the food or even eat it, and then returned it again to the cage. We then released the animal after varying intervals of time, and determined the maximum time for retention of each particular location.

In each of these experimental procedures, we offered food in a completely new situation, so that a new experiment was initiated when the animal ceased going to the previous place of food. Only then did we allow perception of a new location of food.

Perception of a Conditional Feeding Signal. After formation of conditioned feeding behavior in the form of approaching different feeders in response to different auditory signals, we presented a particular feeding signal and then released the animal from the cage after varying intervals following cessation of the sound. The animal had to go to the feeder that had been signaled. In this way we determined the duration of retention of the auditory signal that had been perceived. The source of the sound was either adjacent to the feeder or on the experimental table.

Visual Perception of Food Placed Behind One of the Small Screens Arranged in a Certain Situation, in a Single Visual Field. In front of the cage, small screens were placed at a distance of 2 to 4 m from the cage (Fig. 1, screens 1', 2', 3', and 4'). The food was presented at a distance and then placed behind one of the screens in view of the animal, or the animal was led in front of one of these screens, allowed to smell the food and then led away again.

Emotional Stimuli—Fear. The animal was led to the feeder and while eating was subjected to electrical stimulation as follows: A piece of tin was placed in front of the feeder, the piece of tin and the feeding cage being connected to an outlet via a resistance in such a manner that when the animal stood on the tin and lowered its head into the feeder, it received a small electric shock. With or without a whine, it jumped away from the feeder. Subsequently, the animal became frightened of this feeder. We then studied the duration of the fear of the particular feeder. If the electrical stimulation was carried out simultaneously with a conditional feeding signal, the latter also evoked the emotion of fear.

Retention of Images of Location of Food for a Prolonged Period of Time.
We showed the animal food, allowed the food to be smelled or eaten each
time in a new place in the experimental room or in another room, and then
immediately or after some time led the animal to the vivarium. In some instances after perception of the food, we returned the animal to the cage.
and then led it to the vivarium. After several hours, on the next day, or
after several days, we led it back in a hungry state, and observed where the
dog went first.

Experiments were carried out on mammals (rabbits, cats, monkeys),
fish (goldfish), amphibians (frogs), reptiles (turtles and lizards), and birds
(chickens and pigeons). We also studied the manifestations of memory in
ontogenesis as well as in phylogenesis.

In each experiment, detailed descriptions were made of the overall behavior of the animal, and in addition, moving pictures were taken of all of the
most characteristic behavioral phenomena.

CHARACTERISTICS OF IMAGE MEMORY IN HIGHER VERTEBRATES

Definition of Short-Term and Long-Term Image Memory. In the study of
feeding behavior in higher vertebrates, two forms of image memory were
observed. In the first, the image of the food object perceived is retained in
memory only for some minutes, at the very most, one to two hours. This
occurred if the image was based on a single sensory modality, i.e., visual,
auditory, or vestibular perception of the location of food. We consider this
the manifestation of short-term image memory.

In the other form, upon complex perception in which all sensory modalities, including olfaction and taste, participate, the image of the location
of food is retained for many days or weeks. This is the manifestation of
long-term memory. In view of the characteristic features in the origin of
these and other phenomena of memory, short-term memory will first be considered in detail, and then long-term.

Memory for Visual Perception of Food in Different Situations. As was
indicated under *Methods*, a large series of experiments were carried out on the
retention in memory of the location of food placed in a particular situation
in one of the remote parts of the experimental room. We let the dog perceive
the direction and location of the food in a given situation, and then, after
varying intervals of time, freed the animal so that it could obtain the food.
At a distance of $1\frac{1}{2}$ to 2 m, we showed the bowl of food to the animal, which
was locked in the cage; the food was then moved to a distance of 3 to 7 m

and placed behind one of the screens. After some time the animal was released. On the basis of visual memory, the animal correctly ran to the food, not only after a lapse of some seconds after being shown it, but also after 5 to 15 min. This interval was apparent even in the first test. The position of the animal at the moment of release was of no significance, i.e., it was immaterial whether it was standing or lying down with lowered head as was the direction of pointing of the head or the body. Under all of these conditions, the animal ran correctly to the location of food (Beritashvili, Aivazashvili, and Ordzhonikidze, 1965).

Many authors have studied the maximum delay following visual perception of food. According to Voitonis (1940), the maximum interval in lower simians was 10 to 20 min and in the fox, 7 min. In Konorski's laboratory, the maximum interval was 17 min in dogs and 6 min in cats (Lawicka, 1958).

Memory for Auditory Perception in Dogs, as was indicated under Methods, was studied with eyes both closed and open. With eyes open, a shield was placed in front of the cage, concealing the entire setup from the animal. The laboratory assistant stood somewhere behind the screen, struck the floor with the basin from which the animal had received food, and then, carrying the basin, moved away to the side. The animal went to the source of the noise, within a period of 2 to 8 min, and in the vicinity of the source of noise carried out searching movements. A correct approach to the source of the noise was also observed after a few minutes, if the animal wore a light-tight mask on its head (Beritashvili *et al.*, 1965).

Memory for Vestibular Perception. As was indicated under Methods, an animal with eyes covered (a light-proof mask on the head) was carried in a cage to a particular place a few meters away, and there allowed to smell or eat food. Then in the same way the animal was returned to the cage. After release, it was able to go there even with closed eyes, both immediately as well as some minutes later. In this case we have the perception of the path followed and the location of the food by means of stimulation of the labyrinthine receptors—the semicircular canals and the otolith organs (Beritashvili, 1955; Beritashvili, Aivazashvili, and Ordzhonikidze, 1965). It is characteristic that if the animal was transported in the cage through an angle, it could repeat not only the original path but also could go using a new, shorter path. Consequently, the animal was able to project exactly, in the given surroundings, the final point of the path followed.

In all of these experiments with an individual perception (i.e., based on a single sensory modality), the maximum possible delay was not usually observed in the very first trials. After the first weeks of experiments carried out in our laboratory, the maximum interval in dogs in visual trials ranged from 10 to 20 min, in auditory trials from 6 to 8 min, and in vestibular trials from 3 to 4 min (Beritashvili *et al.*, 1965).

Memory for Visual Perception in Naive Dogs in a New Situation. We usually studied memory for visual perception in those dogs who had already become accustomed to an experimental situation in which they had eaten in a number of places, i.e., from feeders that were placed in specific locations of the particular room, behind large and small screens, i.e., behind which we usually hid the basin with the food. These feeders and screens were sometimes shifted but were always located in the experimental room. It is clear that upon seeing these feeders and screens, a dog could imagine one or more locations of food. It is thus apparent why, when we led a dog into the experimental room, it usually visited all of those feeders behind which it had eaten food in the previous days or weeks.

The following circumstance must play an essential role in the feeding behavior of a dog in the usual experimental room after being shown food in a new location. The dog, leaving the cage, may go not to the latter location, but to the places where it had eaten earlier; for moving about the room under the influence of one or another familiar place of feeding, the image of the new place of feeding may give way to the image of the old place and thus induce the animal's going to the old location of food. This eventuality can readily occur if the dog is allowed to move freely after a long interval of time, such that the image of the new location of food is already dim, i.e., when the psychoneural process of the particular image becomes weaker with time.

In these experiments, in order to establish exactly how long a time the image of the new location of food could be retained and in order to determine the time after which the animal could still go there without deviation to another place of food, the experiments had to be set in a completely new situation, in which the dog had never previously eaten.

Experiments of this specific type were carried out recently in collaboration with Aivazashvili and Natishvili; the results that were found are striking. A dog was led first into the experimental or another room and was allowed to move freely for several minutes, during which time it went around objects and people in the room and sniffed at them. Then it was put into the cage. On the first occasion, the animal was restless and attempted to get out of the cage, but then gradually it became quiet. Screens were placed at different locations in the room; the dog was then shown, at a distance of $1\frac{1}{2}$ to 2 m, a basin with meat, following which, still within sight of the animal, the basin was placed behind one of the screens. Initially, when the cage was opened some minutes following the presentation of the food, the dog, manifesting an innate reflex of freedom, bounded out of the cage, either to the door or to the experimenter. Only after seeing the food did the animal go to it and eat. But gradually it became accustomed to the cage and ceased attempting to get out. After quieting down, the animal went out of the cage calmly when the latter was opened. In this period it was found that if the dog was released 45 to 90 min after the food had been shown and placed behind one of the screens, the animal could go correctly to the food. It did this, however, very slowly and with hesitation and glances to the side; it might return to the cage but did not tarry there, turning around and running in the correct direction, exactly approaching that screen behind which the basin had been placed, and turning toward the latter.

On the same day or on another day, the same experiment was repeated twice; both times the animal went correctly to the food, but very slowly, with hesitation and small deviations to the side (Natishvili, 1966). It was as though the dog was carrying out searching movements according to the reproduced image of the food. Evidently, such a slow goal-directed approach to the location of food characterizes feeding behavior controlled by the visual image of the former under the new conditions. We had previously established this characteristic feature of image behavior in the elaboration of conditioned feeding-movement behavior to indifferent stimuli. On the first experimental day, when this stimulus was presented, the dog did not go immediately to the feeder by way of the shortest path, but slowly and hesitantly. We also established that this feature of behavior characterizes image behavior appearing the first time in a new situation. It was only with the formation and reinforcement of temporary connections that the animal began to move quickly and directly to the feeder that had been signaled (Beritashvili and Tsereteli, 1934). Only when the animal had become accustomed to the particular circumstances of the experiment, with the food that had been presented, did it begin to carry out image behavior quickly and directly. But in this process, the maximum delay decreased significantly as the psychoneural process of the new location of food waned, and hence the dog deviated from the correct path because of images of other locations of food which arose in the familiar circumstance in which food had been presented in different locations.

Under entirely new conditions of the experiment, the visual image of a new location of food was usually not effective after more than $1\frac{1}{2}$ to 2 hr later, and was very rarely evident on the next day.

It should be emphasized that the aforementioned findings by Voitonis, Konorski, Lawicka, and others, as well as by ourselves, of a short interval for visual memory is dependent on the fact that they presented food to the animal many times in the same experimental environment, but sometimes in one and sometimes in another feeder. Accordingly, the image that they generated was of food in all of these feeders; this circumstance interfered with the animals' selection of the correct course directed to a new location of food, after the image for the latter had waned significantly, i.e., when the psychoneural process related to a particular image arose only weakly.

Memory for Visual and Auditory Perception with Prolonged Experience with a Particular Method. When experiments of a given type were carried out systematically over several months, the maximum delay for visual testing became significantly longer. In these experiments, we placed food behind one of the screens within sight of the dog located in the cage. Then we waited 30 min or more, during which we conversed or left the room. The dog lay quietly the entire time and usually dozed. When the cage was opened, the animal, in the majority of cases, went to that screen behind which the food had been placed. After a period of 30 min the animal performed correctly; after longer periods of time, it usually did not go directly to the location of food. Subsequently, in the majority of instances, it did go to the food even an hour after being shown the latter; the longest interval was found to be 2 hr. For such long delays, we usually led the animal to the door or to the vivarium and only after the interval brought it back again (Beritashvili and Aivazashvili, 1967).

After prolonged training, we initially had the impression that there was only a small increase in the maximum interval resulting from prolonged auditory association with the place of food. But if as a preliminary procedure the basin was struck repeatedly while the animal was being fed from it, and if the basin was struck each time the animal ran to the screen, went behind it and ate, then when the sound appeared from some new place, the maximum interval could be prolonged to as much as 15 to 20 min. This finding means that under these conditions the image of the food in the basin is consolidated to such an extent that it is retained and recalled after a lapse of a number of minutes following the sound.

Memory for Complex Perception of the Location of Food. As was indicated under *Methods*, the animal was led by the collar from the cage to a new location of food in the experimental room and allowed to smell the food, following which it was returned to the cage. Upon release after some minutes, the animal ran to the food. We carried out such experiments for some time on various animals (Beritashvili and Tsereteli, 1934; Beritashvili, 1939). In the most recent experiments of this type, carried out with Aivazashvili, we determined the maximum delay for complex perception of food, i.e., including taste and smell, and found that the delay was significantly longer than for isolated perception based on individual sensory modalities. The maximum interval was no longer than two hours for perception of the location of food by means of vision alone, whereas with complex perception, the delayed response could occur on the next day or later, and under certain conditions, such long-term memory could appear even after 18 days. Thus, if food was presented in a completely new location, the dog went directly to that spot after 5, 9, and 18 days, even though there was actually no food there (Beritashvili and Aivazashvili, 1967).

We did not carry out special experiments with longer intervals of time, but it is well known that in the dog the image of the location of food, once having appeared, can be retained for many months. If, for example, the dog under study is brought into the experimental room after a lapse of many months from the time it was last there, the animal immediately goes up to that object at which it had once eaten food (Beritashvili and Tsereteli, 1934).

We specifically studied the role played in long-term memory by different components of complex perception of an object. We found in these experiments, which were carried out in a completely new situation in a new room, that gustatory perception and olfaction during eating constituted the most important contributions to the complex. If a dog was brought to a particular place in one of the rooms and was shown food at a distance of 1 to 2 m, then taken away to the vivarium and the next day brought again in a hungry condition into the adjacent corridor, the dog did not show goal-directed behavior to the previously indicated location of food. If, however, the animal was brought closer to the food and allowed to smell it and then was taken away to the vivarium, then it would run directly and exactly to the location of food, not only on the next day, but also on the third day. The memory of the location of food was retained especially long if the animal was brought to it and allowed to eat. For many days, it would run to this room and run up to the place where it had eaten (Beritashvili and Aivaza-shvili, 1967). This finding indicates that gustatory and olfactory components are of major importance in the complex perception of food for long-term memory.

The vestibular apparatus, which enables the perception of the distance traversed, also participates in the complex perception of the location of food. Experiments showed that dogs without the labyrinths (i.e., after bilateral destruction of the semicircular canals and the otolith organs) and which were also deprived of hearing, exhibited memory after complex perception (i.e., after visual, olfactory, and gustatory perception of food) that was as good as that for normal dogs. According to data of my collaborator, Natishvili, a labyrinthectomized dog went to the location of the complexly perceived food even after several days. From this it can be concluded that perception of the path followed while running to the location of food plays no essential role in long-term retention of the latter.

However, even with complex perception (with the inclusion of taste and olfaction), delayed feeding responses were also observed only after short intervals. This occurred when the dog remained in a constant and unchanged completely silent environment and when it began to drowse after closing its eyes. After 20 to 30 min, the dog might no longer go to the location of the food, but if the environment was changed, e.g., if the dog was led from the room to the vivarium after perceiving the new location of the food and then was brought back again, it would run to the location of food not only after a 20- to 30-min lapse following perception, but even after several hours or on the next day.

Characteristically, correct courses to a new location of food were observed after more prolonged intervals of time at the beginning of an experimental day than when the animal had already eaten in various places in the experimental room on the same day. Following release from the cage, the animal reproduced the image of the food sometimes at one location and sometimes at another, so that it might go to one of the previous locations instead of the new one. This behavior depended in the first instance on the freshness of the image of the location of food, and then on its proximity—the animal ran initially to the closest location of food. This circumstance could interfere strongly with the establishment of the maximum interval after which the animal would still run directly to a new location of food. Thus, these experiments could be carried out only infrequently in the course of a day. Before beginning a new experiment, it was necessary to release the animal from the cage several times; it would initially go around all of these feeding places and then when it had formed a clear image of the absence of food in these locations, it ceased going out of the cage. Only then could a new experiment be started.

This methodological arrangement, however, was not without difficulties. The image of the absence of food was forgotten somewhat earlier than its presence. Thus the animal might visit one and the same place many times in the course of the day or over several days. We noted that quite soon (i.e., on the order of a few minutes) after visiting a location that had no food, the animal began not to go there, but later on invariably visited it anew.

This form of memory, i.e., retention for some 20 min, is usually considered to be short-term. It may concern, separately, memory for visual, auditory, or vestibular perception of an object of vital importance for the animal. But, as was indicated previously, under certain conditions in a completely new circumstance or as a result of extensive training, short-term memory can persist for as long as 1 or even 2 hr.

Memory for complex perception of a location of food, on the other hand, always persists for a number of days, and therefore this phenomenon is usually termed long-term memory. It is true, as has already been mentioned, that if the animal has remained in the same unchanging surroundings after a complex perception for some dozens of minutes, it is unable to go to the location of food after release, 20 to 30 min later. But if subsequently the animal is brought to the yard or to the vivarium and then after some time is brought back again while hungry, it will invariably run to the correct location. Consequently, memory for complex perception of a location of food is basically always long-term in nature.

Variability of Short-Term Memory. Memory for visual perception alone of food is very variable, depending on the particular animal. For a restless, lively dog that prances about in the cage and continually attempts to open the door of the cage during the delay period, the maximum delay is appreciably diminished to 1 to 2 min. However, if the animal quiets down after a light-tight mask is put on, the maximum delay is increased significantly (Beritashvili *et al.*, 1965).

On the other hand, if the dog is quiet, then after 1 or 2 min following its perception of a new location of food, it can be taken out of the cage, walked about the room by its collar for a few moments, during which time it can even be given food, and then taken back into the cage; the animal still responds correctly when released some minutes later (Beritashvili *et al.*, 1965). Under these experimental conditions, the maximum interval can be even greater, since movement of the animal about the room can lead to a reinforced reproduction of the image of the location of the food.

If food is presented at some new location and then a conditional feeding signal is given, the dog may initially run to the feeder that had been signaled, but upon completion of eating at the latter, the animal invariably also runs to the new place of food, either immediately or after returning to the cage (Beritashvili, 1939; Beritashvili and Tsereteli, 1934). Consequently, the delayed response is not interfered with by the prior or alternative feeding behavior.

We also studied delayed responses to conditional feeding signals. Feeding behavior to a particular feeder was first established in response to an auditory signal, and then to another feeder in response to a second auditory signal. The dog was usually placed in a closed cage. After several minutes, the cage was opened from time to time, and the dog released to a feeder and fed there while an indifferent stimulus (e.g., a bell) was sounded. Then the animal was returned to the cage and shut in. If, after a number of such trials, the bell was rung and then the cage was opened, the dog would run to the feeder of its own accord. The same behavior was then established with the other feeder, in response to a tone. Subsequently, the cage was not opened during or immediately following the signal, but only after some time had elapsed. It was found that the feeding behavior appeared not only during the signal or a few seconds later but even after some minutes had elapsed. One or the other feeding signal was then presented, and after varying intervals of time on the order of minutes, the animal was released from the cage. As had already been known, the animal in such cases ran predominantly to the feeder that had been signaled (Lawicka, 1958). In establishing the maximum delay of feeding behavior for the auditory receptor, we found that the maximum delay for feeding behavior for a conditional auditory signal was appreciably longer (i.e., 8 to 12 min) than to the striking of a basin (Beritashvili *et al.*, 1965). Presumably this difference arose from the fact that the conditional feeding sound in such cases was accompanied by systematic feeding for some dozens or a hundred times, i.e., more frequently than to the striking of the basin.

Characteristics of Memory for the Presentation of Food in Different Places under the Same Situation. In the above-described experiments, the food was placed in different remote parts of the room in different situations. As was indicated under Methods, we also carried out a series of experiments in which three or four individual screens were placed in front of the cage at a distance of $1\frac{1}{2}$ to 4 m, which the animal could see all at once. Alongside one of the screens, a bowl with food was shown and then was placed behind the same screen. On the very first day of the experiment, it was found that with the first presentation of the food behind one of the screens, the dog ran directly there after an interval as long as 10 to 20 min. After being fed behind another screen, however, the animal went directly to the feeder only after a very short period of 3 to 5 min; if the period was longer, the dog first went around the other screens and then approached the food.

If the dog was led to one of the screens and there shown food and allowed to smell it, then the animal was observed to go directly to the feeder after a prolonged interval of 20 to 30 min only at the beginning of an experimental day, i.e., only on the first trial of the day. But if the dog were taken to food behind the other screens, then the interval after which it would run directly to the feeder was shorter. For example, one of the dogs went directly after 10 min, but after 20 or 25 min it went around other screens before approaching the food. The closer the cage stood to the screen, the less the maximum interval. On one occasion the screen stood at a distance of 4 m in front of the cage, for which the maximum interval was 15 min, whereas for a distance of $1\frac{1}{2}$ m, the maximum interval was decreased to 5 min (Beritashvili and Aivazashvili, 1968).

The same dog, which after long experience of being shown and sniffing food in different situations went correctly after a delay of 30 to 60 min, was not able to go correctly to the feeding screen even after 20 min if the latter was placed among other screens.

ORIGIN OF SHORT-TERM IMAGE MEMORY

Structural Basis of the Psychoneural Process of Perception and Imagery. Psychoneural memory is directly based on the perception and establishment of the image of the external world. In order to understand the phenomenon of psychoneural memory correctly, the psychoneural process of perception and the origin of images must first be understood correctly. We will thus consider the nature of this neural process.

Perception of the food object occurs in the context of its surroundings, e.g., the screen behind which the basin with food is located as well as the general aspect of the experimental room in which the screen is located, or in which the noise of striking the basin containing food occurs. According to our conception, the perception of all of this occurs as a result of excitation of stellate sensory neurons with a pericellular axonal network (see Beritashvili, *Neural Mechanisms of Higher Vertebrate Behavior*, 1965). We call these neurons of the cortex, sensory neurons, for they generate, upon excitation of afferent impulses, the sensation of light, color, sound, touch, etc. They are basically found in layer IV of the primary area of the perceiving region of the cortex, on which terminate the afferent thalamic pathways from receptors, i.e., in the primary area of the perceiving region.

For visual perception, the corresponding area in the dog is area 17 of Brodmann, which occupies the medial and dorsal surface of the occipital region. For auditory perception, the primary area in the dog occupies the middle third of the ectosylvian gyrus. The same afferent pathways simultaneously excite the internuncial pyramidal neurons (small pyramidal neurons, the axons of which do not leave the cortex) and transmitting stellate neurons (stellate neurons, the axons of which do not leave the cortex and do not ramify around cells, but terminate on pyramidal neurons) in the primary area. From these neurons, the excitation is transmitted to association pyramidal neurons (larger pyramidal neurons, the axons of which pass from the cortex into the subcortical white matter and then return again to the cortex, thus interconnecting different parts of the cortex) of the same primary area, which is in turn connected with the association neurons of the secondary area of the same sensory region and also with similar neurons of other sensory regions. As is well known, for the visual region the secondary area consists of area 18 and 19, and for the auditory, the sylvian and suprasylvian area (Beritashvili, 1961, 1963).

The secondary area, however, also receives impulses from the receptors directly, by the corresponding specific system, and by nonspecific pathways, through the reticular formation and the ascending reticular system. For example, it is well known from morphologic and oscillographic studies that afferent pathways of the retina terminate in the dog not only in cortical area 17 but also in area 18 (the suprasylvian gyrus); in area 7 (the middle suprasylvian gyrus); in areas 21 and 22 (the posterior ectosylvian and suprasylvian gyri); and also to a slight degree in the cruciate gyrus. It has been established that this transmission of visual impulses originates by way of thalamocortical pathways from "association" thalamic nuclei which are excited by collaterals from primary visual pathways (Buser and Borenstein, 1959).

It has been shown morphologically that there are also direct centripetal connections of the retina with the cortex, centripetal fibers terminating predominantly as axosomatic connections with cortical neurons of different types in layers III, V, and VI (Skerbitskii and Shkol'nik-Yarros, 1964). Oscillographic studies with stimulation of visual pathways also indicate that they are distributed in nonvisual regions, e.g., in the suprasylvian gyrus (Vastola, 1961).

The Significance of Closed Neural Circuits in the Origin of Memory. Simultaneous excitation of the primary and secondary areas of the perceiving regions, as well as of the adjacent association regions presumably results in the establishment of two-way neural connections, i.e., complex closed neural circuits among neurons of all of these regions of the cortex. Accordingly, their excitation does not cease immediately after perception, i.e., after the external influence; the excitation may circulate for many seconds in neural circuits, with a frequency of 50 to 100 per sec or higher. This persistence, of course, strengthens and prolongs the activity of their synapses. Moreover, as is well known, distinct structural changes are observed in synapses after more or less prolonged excitation, in the main in the presynaptic endings. Shmirnov, D'yachkova, and Manteifel (1968) found that stimulation of the optic nerve of the frog results in an increase in the quantity of synaptic vesicles in the optic tectum, the vesicles not infrequently filling the entire portion of the ending, adjoining the presynaptic membrane. This new formation of synaptic vesicles appears gradually in the course of rhythmic stimulation of the nerve and becomes noticeable as early as 3 to 8 sec after initiation of stimulation. After cessation of the stimulation, the increased quantity of vesicles does not disappear immediately but persists for several minutes, gradually returning to the resting quantity and distribution.

It is also known that with prolonged rhythmic stimulation, the quantity and even the size of synaptic vesicles increases in presynaptic terminals in other neural centers. The vesicles accumulate at the presynaptic membrane, a significant portion of them being adjacent to it (Fujimoto, 1966; D'yachkova, Hamori, and Fedina 1967). Analogous studies have been carried out on the cerebral hemispheres, but not with the same detail as in the abovementioned experiments in the frog. Thus, D'yachkova (1964) observed that with prolonged generalized excitation of the cortex in the monkey, the number of synaptic vesicles increased as they move toward the presynaptic membrane. In some instances, at the sites of contact of vesicles with the membrane, the membrane itself was deficient, the zone of the synaptic vesicles appearing to communicate directly with the synaptic cleft. Sometimes the cleft itself was partially or completely filled with osmophillic material.

It should be noted that synaptic vesicles must be formed in neural centers, in particular in neuronal circuits of the cortex, not only during the excitation that activates them but also subsequently, as long as the reverberation of excitation in these circuits persists. Thus, the longer the reverberation, the greater the accumulation of the vesicles. The prevailing concept is that the active substance or mediator in the form of acetylcholine is secreted from these vesicles, which then traverses the presynaptic membrane and the synaptic space, resulting in depolarization of the postsynaptic membrane. Prolonged synaptic potentiation thus ensues, which is functionally expressed as a prolonged increase in cellular excitability.

Upon cessation of the reverberation of excitation, the vesicles and the mediator are gradually dissipated and accordingly, after some time, the quantity of vesicles and their distribution within the presynaptic endings become normal. At that time the level of cellular excitability returns to normal.

It is known from the results of Roitbak (1953, 1960) that in acute experiments with anesthetized cats, stimulation of a small part of the cortex results in an increase of excitability in neighboring regions, which can persist for 3 to 5 min, according to Okudzhava (1959). An increased excitability can persist for 20 min or more in chronic experiments following even brief tetanic stimulation using implanted electrodes. This functional change of an increase of excitability in the cerebral cortex must also occur as a result of the secretion of mediator from vesicles. Thus, it can be presumed that the same prolonged increase of excitability must occur in the neuronal circuits of the cortex upon the perception of a location of food. This increase of excitability evidently constitutes the principal basis of short-term image memory, i.e., on the order of minutes. In this period, not only can the particular object (or a part of it) suffice for the reproduction of the image of the location of the food, but even some extraneous stimulus that results in an orienting response can also be effective, owing to radiation of the excitation in the cerebral cortex with resulting activation of the neural circuits involved in the earlier perception of the food object. If in this period, a hungry animal is placed in surroundings that are the same as those in which food had been perceived, the animal will invariably go to the correct spot, in accordance with the corresponding image.

The image of the location of food under certain conditions is reproduced after many minutes. This phenomenon occurs not only after perception of the food that involves olfaction and taste, but even after a single visual perception of the location of the food. For example, after visual perception of food in a completely new location, the reproduction of the image of this spot, accompanied by the appropriate behavior, can occur after 1 to 2 hr or even after 24 hr. Such a prolonged retention of the image of the place of food could hardly be dependent on the above-mentioned increase of excitability due to a mediator. It must be presumed that for such a prolonged delay of feeding behavior, the reproduction of the image of the location of food is dependent on the formation, during the reverberation of excitation, of a special type of active protein in the association pyramidal neurons within the cortex. As will be detailed below, in considering long-term memory, it is presumed that the active protein formed at the time of perception migrates into the postsynaptic part of the pyramidal cell that is activated at the particular moment. Presumably, this protein persists at the latter site for a long time, and participates directly in the functioning of the membrane, facilitating the transmission of excitation across the postsynaptic membrane when the synapse is excited chemically or electrically. This facilitatory effect of the active protein on the postsynaptic membrane must be recognized as one of the principal sources of the origin and retention of increased excitability in the activated neuronal circuits over a long period of time.

As long as the excitation circulates in neural circuits, it will activate sensory elements that are functionally connected with them. As is well known, association fibers arriving at a given part of the cortex from other parts of it terminate not only on pyramidal association and internuncial neurons that form closed circuits, but by means of their collaterals also terminate on sensory stellate cells of layer IV and on intermediary pyramidal neurons in layers II and III which in turn give off axons to the same sensory cells. Thus, after the excitatory activity ceases, a subjective reflection of the perceived object can persist in the form of the image of the object. Since a particular object is perceived together with its surroundings, the image is projected in the same surroundings as originally. When the given neural circuits are excited, efferent cortical neurons of the orienting response that are connected with them are also excited, and hence the head and the eyes turn in the direction of the projected image, which leads to the appropriate feeding behavior.

When the excitation ceases to circulate because of fatigue or inhibition of certain links in the neural circuit, the image disappears. But as long as the condition of synaptic potentiation with increased excitability in the association neurons persists, the particular neural circuits can easily be excited again by the same object or a part of it, or even by its surroundings, thus evoking anew the image of the location of the food. As a consequence, orienting movements in the direction of the location of food can ensue.

It was mentioned above that if visual perception of the location of food occurs under completely new circumstances, the image of this location can reappear not only after 15 to 20 min but also after an appreciably longer delay, of approximately two hours or even longer. As has been indicated previously, such a prolonged delay depends on the fact that under such circumstances, images of food in other locations do not arise which would distract the animal from the particular new image. Thus, the animal can go to the location of food as long as the increased excitability in the given association neuronal circuits persists, or more precisely, as long as the active protein that had been formed in the perceiving areas during the perception of the given location of food remains at some high level.

Further, we noted previously that in systematic experiments in which a new location of food was shown at a distance repeatedly for a number of weeks, the maximum interval of the feeding response was also prolonged from 15 or 20 min to 2 hr. Presumably, this phenomenon of practice is related to the circumstance that with repeated visual perception of the basin with food, there is an increase in the quantity of active protein formed in the association neural circuits participating in the retention of the image of the basin of food and of the place where the latter was located. On the other hand, under these experimental conditions, the animal usually received food only at locations where food had previously been placed in sight of the animal. A negative relationship was therefore established by the animal to all other locations where it had eaten food earlier; upon seeing them, images of the absence of food in them must have been generated, since the animal had visited these earlier locations where there was no food.

The Role of Adaptation to the Surroundings in Relation to Memory. The maximum delay of recall is dependent not only on the duration of the reverberating excitation and hence the synaptic potentiation or the period of increased excitability, but also on those external conditions which were mentioned above, such as the familiarity or unfamiliarity of the surroundings, and the total extent in time of the same experiment in which food is exhibited, or the basin is struck. The adaptation of the animal to the surroundings is also of major importance since the animal may cease to be excited by the surroundings and thus cease to reproduce the image of the location of the food. In experiments with delayed responses after feeding in an unusual place, after food is exhibited, or after the basin is struck in an unusual place, if the external circumstances in the experimental room remained quite unchanged, the animal did not experience any unusual stimuli from these surroundings. Thus, the animal ceased to respond to the situation with an orienting response, either externally, such as movement of the head, or internally, such as visceral activity.

When the orienting response to one and the same repeated external influence disappears, the same process must occur in the central nervous system as occurs during extinction of a conditioned reflex. Presumably, in such extinction, subcortical inhibitory mechanisms under the influence of corticofugal impulses, i.e., the thalamic reticular formation, are included, which depresses both the activity of the cortex and that of subcortical motor mechanisms. This effect is indicated on the one hand by the appearance of intensified dendritic electrical activity over the entire cortex which, according to the concept of dendritic inhibition, produces a general inhibition of the cortex, and on the other hand by the animal's becoming quiet and motionless, with the cessation of orienting responses: the animal lies down, lowers its head, and closes its eyes (Beritashvili, 1961). The very same processes occur upon extinction of the orienting reflex (Roitbak, 1956; Sokolov, 1960; and others). In this generalized inhibition, a more important role may be played by the hippocampus, since it is well known that electrical stimulation of it by implanted electrodes evokes a generalized inhibition both of feeding and of defensive conditioned and unconditioned reflexes, as well as of orienting responses to external stimuli. On the other hand, bilateral destruction of the hippocampus leads to hyperkinesia, i.e., an enhanced manifestation of both conditioned and orienting responses (Lissak and Grastyan, 1957; Grastyan and Karmos, 1962; Tevzadze, 1968).

It is clear that in such suppression of cortical activity resulting from activation of the hippocampus, the association neurons of the circuits that activate sensory stellate neurons and thus result in the reproduction of the image of the location of the food must also cease to be excited.

If the situation of the experiment is disturbed, i.e., if the dog is taken out of the experimental room for a few minutes, then of course this generalized inhibition disappears. It is also clear that if the animal is then returned again, it begins to mainfest the orienting response anew. Therefore, under the influence of the altered situation of the experiment, the dog immediately reproduces the image of that screen behind which the food had been placed, and invariably goes there, either directly or after visiting other feeding places. This behavior is especially evident if a dog, having failed because of adaptation to go to a location of food which had previously been perceived, is then led out into the courtyard some minutes after its release. If then some time lapses and the animal is brought again into the experimental room, it may go directly to the appropriate feeding place. It is clear that this behavior results from the appearance of an orienting response and the renewal of the image of the feeding place as a consequence of the disappearance of adaptation to the experimental situation.

Thus the maximum delay for visual or auditory perception is dependent on many factors, in particular on the circumstance of how rapidly adaptation of the animal to the surroundings ensues, i.e., how quickly the orienting response to the particular surroundings is extinguished.

Memory for the Absence of Food in a Specific Location. An animal retains a memory not only of the presence of food in a specific location, i.e., the image of it and its location amid the particular surroundings, but also a memory of its absence in a given location. If a dog has eaten all of the food in some location to which it is unaccustomed, then for a time it will not go there or will go only very slowly, and turn around before reaching it. Or, the animal may go up to the location of the food, and, without even sniffing at it, immediately turn around. Characteristically, however, the animal may go there again after some minutes. A hungry dog may repeat from day to day the feeding behavior to the same place at which it had once eaten (Beritashvili, 1939), but it will not go twice to the same empty location after a short interval of time.

In this way, the regulation of feeding behavior by the image of the absence of food appears only for a short time, i.e., in the range of a few minutes, when measured under the same experimental conditions. What is the origin of this phenomenon of memory?

First of all, we should say that in a hungry animal the perception of food is accompanied by a pleasant sensation, and its absence in a familiar location is accompanied by an unpleasant one. These emotional conditions result from activation of a specific neural substratum in the limbic system. The paleocortex participates together with the neocortex in the feeding behavior on each occasion and, as is well known, with unpleasant emotional excitation from electrical sitmulation by means of implanted electrodes of certain parts of the paleocortex, or with the appearance of unpleasant emotional behavior under the influence of the external surroundings, together with excitation of a specific neuronal complex in different parts of the brain, general inhibition of all remaining parts of the brain occurs, so that the appearance of other behavioral responses becomes impossible.

It must be supposed that in vertebrates, the image of the absence of food in a familiar location is accompanied by an unpleasant emotional reaction and therefore the animal avoids this place. But let us suppose that the unpleasant feeling which arises upon reproduction of the image of the absence of food disappears earlier than the pleasant feeling with the image of presence of food, and that this is presumably a natural characteristic of psychoneural organization of the archipaleocortex; this would mean that the psychoneural circuits in the limbic system that give rise to an unpleasant sensation upon the image of the absence of food cease being activated somewhat earlier than those neural circuits of the pleasant sensation of the image of the presence of food. This circumstance must be of prime biological significance—the animal does not forget for a long time a location of food perceived on a single occasion.

The Psychoneural Bases of Variability of Short-Term Memory. We have considered the origin of short-term memory in the presence of the location of food in various situations. It was mentioned previously that if in a given experimental day all screens that hid the food were the same and remain fixed, always in view of the animal, the correct, direct course to the food screen could appear with the first trial, usually still after a delay of 20 min or more. But later, if the food was placed behind one of these screens, the dog went directly to this screen after an interval of only 3 to 5 min. If the animal was brought behind the screen and allowed to scent the food, the dog responded correctly on the first trial after a delay of up to 20 min or more. For subsequent trials with delays of more than 10 min, the animal usually ran to the screens and went around them with searching movements and thus found the food.

This variability of the interval of the external manifestation of short-term memory we explain as follows. In the presence of a place of food in a particular situation, i.e., if the food screen is placed in a given field of vision, two aspects in the behavior of the animal must be distinguished: the image of the direction to the food screen and the image of the screen itself. From experiment to experiment, the image of the direction changes, but the image of the screen itself remains the same. Moreover, all of the screens that were used from day to day to cover the food constituted conditional signals for feeding behavior, and therefore the dog in general ran to the screens after being released. The correct direction was determined by the location of that screen behind which the food presented had been placed the last time. It is evident then that the excitation of reverberating circuits, which, because of their synaptic potentiation with a corresponding period of increased excitability, determines the image of the direction to the food screen, diminishes somewhat in the course of time. Therefore, appropriate orienting behavior ceases to be evoked and hence the animal runs indiscriminantly to the screen standing directly in front of it, after which it goes around the remaining screens until it finds the food.

As was indicated above, in restless dogs the maximum delay for both visual and auditory perception of a food object can be significantly less. This decrease must depend on the fact that in very restless dogs, in association with vigorous movements and strong emotional excitation, cortical pyramidal neurons must be subject to intense inhibition, primarily from a strongly activated part of the reticular formation.

Therefore, association neural circuits of the image of the location of food, also being inhibited for some time after perception, are no longer distinguished amid the general background of heightened activity. This circumstance must also lead to a pronounced decrease of the maximum delay for the feeding response directly to a new place of food, and for evoking an adequate orienting response.

However, in such restless dogs, the maximum delay to auditory perception (of the striking of the basin) significantly increases after wearing a mask on the head and quieting down. Wearing the mask on the head results in an inhibitory effect on locomotion and on movement in general. Moreover, with closed eyes, orienting behavior to visual stimuli ceases. This calming down in turn must lead to a diminution in the inhibitory effect on the cerebral cortex thereby facilitating the reproduction of the image of the location of food, so that the animal gives an appropriate delayed response.

But characteristically, if the excited state in the dog arises as a result of individually acquired aggressive behavior such as that which occurs when a cat is seen, then there is no significant effect on the delayed feeding response. If a cat is brought close to the cage of the dog, the latter begins to bark at it, paws at the cage as though to escape from it. This behavior can last for minutes, but if the dog is shown food in the new place, even with such violent behavior, after the cage is opened, the animal will run in the first instance to the place of food, and not to the cat. From this it follows that in a hungry dog, such an aggressive individually acquired response is easily suppressed by the psychoneural process of the image of the location of the food, or more precisely, by the consequent activation of the integrated mechanism of feeding behavior.

We also indicated previously that if after visual or auditory perception of food in a new place, the dog is taken by the collar and is quietly transferred into the experimental room and even given food there, then this will not interfere with the delay of the feeding behavior followig the animal's release. It is evident that such movement by the dog in the given situation results in enhanced perception of it by the animal. In this reinforcement, not only are neural circuits of the particular situation activated, but also the neural circuits of the image of the location of food which are connected with such circuits, with the effect that the maximum delay of recall can even be increased.

Thus, that phenomenon of memory which is commonly called short-term memory is dependent on circulation of excitation in closed neural circuits of association neurons connecting the primary perceiving areas with secondary zones or other association regions, and on the ensuing synaptic potentiation, i.e., on a period of increased excitability, and still further, on the absence of adaptation to the experimental environment. But, as was indicated above, more or less prolonged retention in memory of the image of the perceived external object must be dependent on the formation of a special active protein in the excited postsynaptic parts of the association pyramidal cells. It must be presumed that this protein persists for a long time and is essential for the better function of the postsynaptic membrane, thus facilitating transfer of excitation. In this same way, it facilitates reproduction of the image of the given object after a greater or lesser prolonged time following its perception.

CORTICAL SUBSTRATES OF IMAGE MEMORY

The Significance of Secondary Zones of Perceiving Areas and the Proreal Gyri. We carried out a special study of the association neurons that participate in the retention of delayed responses to visual perception in the dog. We found that following bilateral destruction of the secondary visual areas (areas 18 and 19), short-term memory for visual perception of a food place was absent in the first postoperative weeks. The animal, however, was able to see quite adequately; if it was shown food, it went to the latter. But if the food was concealed from the animal's eyes, it would not go there after 10 to 15 sec. Such disturbance of short-term memory to visual perception of food subsequently recovered, but very slowly—over the course of several months.

Conditioned feeding behavior in the form of running to a specific feeder in response to a specific visual signal was preserved. But again, on the first trial after the operation, the dog went to the feeder only during the signal itself. If the signal ceased and the dog was released from the cage a minute later, it might not go to the feeder that had been signaled. Later on, however, after a lapse of 1 to 2 months, the ability of making a delayed response to a conditional signal was restored.

It is characteristic that this disturbance of short-term memory following removal of the secondary visual area is apparent only for visual perception; memory to auditory perception, for example, remains unaltered. However, auditory perception itself is disturbed if the secondary auditory area (the suprasylvian, anterior ectosylvian, and sylvian gyri) is removed bilaterally. In fact, short-term memory is disturbed for both auditory and vestibular perception (Beritashvili and Aivazashvili, 1958).

In all of these cases of bilateral removal of the secondary zones, long-term memory for complex perception of a food object and its location is not disturbed. Evidently, removal of these secondary visual or auditory areas cannot influence gustatory and olfactory perception of food, which play an essential role in long-term memory.

Unilateral and bilateral removal of the primary visual area (area 17) was also carried out. This operation resulted in disturbance of visual perception. Upon the elaboration of conditional feeding behavior to a picture of a specific animal which was projected on a screen, the experimental dog could not distinguish the image of one animal from that of another. The dog uniformly ran to the feeding place following any projection on the screen. Prior to operation, the animal responded differentially not only to figures of different animals, but a part of a given figure could even be differentiated from the whole (Sikharulidze, 1962).

Of the greatest significance in relation to the retention in memory of perceived objects is the prefrontal region of the cortex, more exactly the proreal gyri. Unilateral removal of the latter was found to have no influence on memory, but bilateral removal, as is well known from the data of many other authors (Jacobsen, 1935; Konorski and Lawicka, 1959; Rosvold and Mishkin, 1961; Mishkin, 1964; Brutkovskii, 1966, and others), strongly interferes with image memory. The interference is such that memory is disturbed in relation to retention of images perceived by sensory organs individually as well as for complex perception in which taste and olfaction participate (Aivazashvili, 1968).

If the proreal gyrus is injured only partially, the disturbance of short-term memory is apparent for 1 to 2 months and then is completely restored. But if the removal of the proreal gyrus is complete on both sides, memory is disturbed for a long time. Its restoration in the course of time does occur, but even after a long lapse of time it does not return to normal.

Disturbance of long-term memory upon injury to a part of the proreal gyrus is not observed, but if it is removed completely, memory is significantly disturbed. Long-term memory of the location of food does occur for several days following perception, i.e., it if still observed after a lapse of 3 to 5 days, but not later (Aivazashvili, 1968). In the normal animal we observed it even after 18 days.

Thus, the proreal gyri are of essential significance for prolonged retention of image memory for food objects.

The Role of the Temporal Lobes in Memory. In the phenomenon of memory in man, the temporal lobe is of essential importance, as Penfield (1954) has pointed out. Electrical stimulation of the temporal lobe evokes visual and auditory perceptions from previous experience such that stimulation of a specific part results in specific recollections.

The participation of the temporal lobes in the phenomenon of memory has also been established in monkeys. Following bilateral removal of the inferior temporal region, differential visual perceptions are disturbed and delayed responses that are related to visual projection areas are absent (Mishkin and Pribram, 1954). It is known that following bilateral destruction of the posterior temporal region, differential auditory perceptions are also disturbed significantly (Weiskrantz and Mishkin, 1958).

But in general, experiments on monkeys following removal of the temporal lobes have been carried out in relation to remembering learned movements. It has thus been established that following operation, learned movements associated with specific visual and auditory as well as with olfactory, tactile, and gustatory stimuli are impaired (Pribram and Bagshaw, 1953; Mishkin and Pribram, 1954; Goldberg, Diamond, and Neff, 1957, 1958; Wilson, 1957). But these studies did not bring out the ability of recollection on the basis of reproduction of an image of a place of food, under conditions of free movement.

This type of study was first carried out by Natishvili and Sikharulidze (1968). They removed the sylvian gyrus from the temporal lobes in dogs, together with the middle and posterior parts of the ectosylvian gyrus bilaterally. In all of the animals, conditioned-reflex approach to a given feeding location had been elaborated to a specific sound; approach to another feeding place had been conditioned by a particular figure of an animal (rabbit, cat, or dog) projected onto a screen. After operation, a pronounced disturbance of behavior was observed. The dogs were immobile, inert, and timid and all appeared to be blind. Some became aggressive. After 2 or 3 weeks following the operation, they could see only at a very close distance, up to 50 or 80 cm. After 3 or 4 months they saw well at a distance of 2 to 3 m, but could not see at greater distances. After several months, their behavior changed for the better; they moved freely about the laboratory, and fear and aggressive responses disappeared. They went into the cage in response to a command, and they began to respond to the conditional signal by movement toward the respective feeder. However, fine differentiation of auditory signals and differentiation of pictures were not restored until after 3 or 4 months.

At the same time, image memory was severely disturbed. For almost an entire month, the animal went out of the cage in response to the conditional signals only during the latter or within 10 or 15 sec afterwards. The maximum of the delayed response to the conditional signal increased gradually. Thus, after the third or fourth month, the animal went correctly to the feeder for 3 or 4 min following the conditional signal, whereas prior to operation the corresponding interval was 10 to 12 min. For visually perceived food locations, the maximum delay was 6 min, whereas before operation it exceeded 20 min. The maximum interval for labyrinthine reception in the normal animal was 5 to 6 min, but after operation, 2 to 3 min.

In view of the fact that a specific visual area is located in this region, which receives afferent impulses predominantly from the homolateral primary visual area and also, to a lesser degree, from the visual area of the contralateral hemisphere, it is as though this region constituted a secondary visual area (Batting and Rosvold, 1963).

Short-term memory for complex stimuli was also disturbed. Operated dogs made their way to the feeding place for only 9 to 10 min after its initial perception, whereas normally this could be done even after 40 min. Consequently, following removal of the inferior temporal lobe, the delayed response to olfactory perception was also significantly disturbed. What was striking, however, was that long-term memory was in fact not disturbed. The animal correctly found its way in the last instance to the perceived place of food on the second and the third day, and even 2 or 3 weeks after opeation, at a time when short-term memory was limited to a few minutes (Natishvili and Sikharulidze, 1968).

American authors, in contradistinction to Natishvili and Sikharulidze, did not always observe a disturbance of delayed responses to visual stimuli.

This difference, evidently, is determined by the difference between the methods used, namely they observed only very short delays on the order of 15 to 30 sec when using the Wisconsin apparatus for the delayed responses. In this apparatus, the openings within which the food is placed are located in a single field of vision of the monkey and are situated close to one another at a distance of 10 to 13 cm. Thus, the openings were at a distance from the monkey such that the latter could obtain the food by reaching the hand out of the cage.

Thus, bilateral lesions of the inferior temporal lobes resulted in a significant worsening of short-term memory, without particular disturbance of long-term memory.

Presumably these parts of the temporal lobes, located between the visual, auditory, and vestibular projection areas, constitute a generalized association area for visual, auditory, and vestibular perception, and also, in view of the connections with the prefrontal region, for olfactory and gustatory perceptions. Evidently, both the differentiation of all of these perceptions individually, and their integration, whether occurring simultaneously or sequentially, take place by means of association neurons of these parts of the temporal lobes. Histological studies have shown that these temporal regions are connected bilaterally both with the secondary visual areas and with the prefrontal region (Nauta, 1964). Moreover, it is known that destruction of the proreal gyrus leads to degeneration of association fibers, in particular in the temporal lobes (Mikeladze and Kiknadze, 1965). From all of this it follows that the temporal regions mentioned must also be connected with the proreal gyri by means of association neurons. *Consequently, it can be stated that each phenomenon of memory is dependent on the combined activity of the secondary areas, the proreal gyri, and the inferior temporal lobes.*

The Role of the Hippocampus in Memory. The question of the role played by the hippocampus in the process of memory has become the object of special studies, after clinical observations that patients with disturbances of memory were characterized by degenerative changes in the hippocampus. The latter changes were especially related to changes of memory for recent events. Alterations of memory were also noted following those neurosurgical operations in which the hippocampus was damaged for one or another reason. It has been noted, for example, that following operative removal of the hippocampus and the hippocampal gyri bilaterally, such recent memory is lost so that patients do not remember the course of experience of all that occurred to them before the operation. Memory for the remote past, however, was not lost (Penfield and Milner, 1958). Cases of so-called retrograde amnesia are well known in which, following operation on the hippocampus, there is a sharp diminution of memory to those events which had taken place in the few months prior to operation. Thus, e.g., following operation, one patient was quite unable to remember the number of the ward in which he had been, but remembered very well the name of a street on which he had lived many years previously, in childhood. Following the operation, he could play tennis as well as before (McCleary and Moore, 1965). Cases have also been noted in which, following bilateral damage to the hippocampus, dementia developed (Glees and Griffith, 1952). On the other hand, cases are also known in which, despite serious disturbance of the hippocampus, the patient retains a high development of the intellect, without any apparent impairment whatsoever (Nathan and Smith, 1950).

It is evident that disorders of memory for the most recent events is noted in those patients in which the hippocampus is damaged together with injury to the medial parts of the temporal cortex (Scoville and Milner, 1957). That there is also necessarily damage to other brain structures when the hippocampus is damaged is indicated by the following fact. It has been noted that there are degenerative changes in the hippocampus in the development of amnesia in Korsakov's syndrome. On the other hand, it has become clear that amnesia in Korsakov syndrome occurs only when there are also changes in thalamic structures as well (Victor, 1964).

A further, at first glance, paradoxical point should be mentioned: amnesia, not unlike that which has been described as a result of damage to the hippocampus, occurs also upon electrical stimulation of the uninjured hippocampus (Bickford et al., 1958). This fact evidently indicates that both a decrease and an excessive increase of activity of the hippocampus is reflected in the function of memory.

Experiments on animals, although still insufficient and not verified in detail, show a variable picture of changes of behavior following damage or removal of the hippocampus. In the rat, some difficulties in the solution of maze tasks (i.e., finding the correct path) are noted following bilateral lesions of the hippocampus (Kaada, Rasmussen, and Kveim, 1961).

Observations on cats have shown that bilateral lessions of the hippocampus result in a disturbance of conditioned reflex activity. Recent memory in the form of delayed responses to visual and auditory perception of food are also strongly disturbed, but all of these defects last only for 1 or 2 months (Nutsubidze, 1963). From these data, it is difficult to judge the role of the hippocampus in the phenomenon of memory for perception of the external world. The hippocampus undoubtedly is connected bilaterally with the neocortex, probably primarily with the visual and auditory perceiving regions by thalamic nuclei and the reticular formation. Therefore, bilateral damage to it, in the first instance, necessarily affects the activity of the neocortex, in particular, in relation to memory. According to preliminary experiments by Dzidzishvili and Ungiadze (1969), if the dorsal hippocampus is completely removed, resulting in a generalized inhibition bilaterally, short-term image memory appears to be improved. On the other hand, following bilateral removal of the ventral hippocampus, stimulation of which in the normal improves short-term memory, there is a significant deterioration of memory. It is also evident that the reticular formation has an effect on memory. Activation of the dorsal portion of the reticular formation probably results in an inhibition of the cortex and therefore bilateral removal of it has a facilitatory effect on cortical activity. The reverse, i.e., an inhibitory effect, results from removal of the ventral region, for in the normal, this region facilitates cortical activity (Dzidzishvili and Ungiadze, 1969, personal communication).

However, generally speaking, the question of the role of the hippocampus in the function of memory requires further detailed study. On the other hand, it can be presumed that association neurons connect the hippocampal gyri with the secondary areas bilaterally, the proreal gyri, and also the inferior temporal lobes. On each occasion of visual or auditory perception of food, all of these neural pathways undergo reverberatory excitation with the attendant synaptic potentiation and increase of excitability. This results, on the one hand, in the activation of sensory neurons that produce an image of the feeding place that is projected externally, and on the other hand, in an activation of efferent projecting neurons which result in an appropriate orienting response and the consequent orienting movement toward the feeding place.

Neuronal Organization of the Proreal Gyri and Their Connections with Other Parts of the Brain. The proreal gyrus is characteristically different from the perceiving areas. According to data of Kiknadze and Mikeladze (1968), it does not contain stellate cells, and consequently, no layer IV can be distinguished, rather, it contains predominantly pyramidal cells. Layer II consists of pyramids with comparatively small branching processes and short axons, whereas the medium-sized pyramids of layer II and the upper substratum of layer III are more pear-shaped than triangular in form. Clearly formed medium and large pyramids with large apical dendrites and a thick bundle of basal processes are distributed in layers III and V, but less commonly in layer VI, where polygonal cells predominate. In addition to pyramidal cells in the proreal gyrus, spindle-shaped cells (found most frequently in layer II) and triangular-shaped cells with rather long processes extending beyond the limits of the same layer (Fig. 2) are frequently encountered. Evidently, the main mass of these cells in layers II and III participate in the formation of functional systems corresponding to perceptions that have been retained for a long time, thus effecting the reproduction of the image of the perceived object.

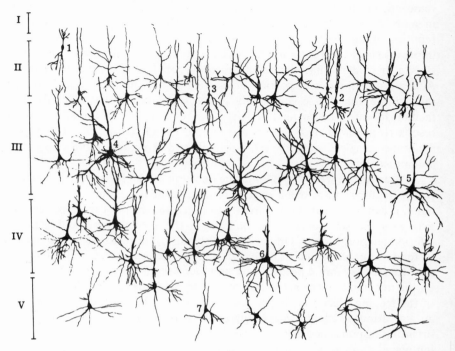

Fig. 2. Neuronal structure of the proreal gyrus (gyrus proreus) of the cerebral cortex in the dog. Cells 8, 9, 10, and 11 are small pyramids; 12 and 13 are intermediate pear-shaped pyramids; 4, 5, 6, 16, and 17 are large pyramids; 1, 2, and 3 are spindle-shaped cells; 7, 14, and 15 are triangular cells; 18 is a polygonal cell (Kiknadze and Mikeladze, 1968).

In the proreal gyrus, there are large pyramidal cells reminiscent of Betz cells (note cells 4, 5, 6, 16, and 17 in Fig. 2), the axons of which presumably give rise to extrapyramidal pathways.

The neuronal organization of the secondary visual area is approximately the same as that in the proreal gyrus. The large proliferation in layer III depends almost entirely on the number of pyramidal cells. The very narrow layer IV has a small quantity of stellate cells. On these cells, presumably, depends the perception of light and darkness following removal of the primary visual area.

Efferent Connections of the Proreal Gyrus. Neural connections of the proreal gyrus with subcortical structures have been repeatedly studied by various authors by the method of degeneration of efferent pathways. Degenerative changes have been observed in the temporal lobes, the caudate nucleus, the amygdaloid complex, the hypothalamus, the thalamus, subthalamus, tegmentum, midbrain, and in general in the limbic system (Auer, 1956; Nauta, 1964; Gragg, 1965; Webster, 1965; and Rinvik, 1966).

At this point it is relevant to mention some very recent data from the results of a study by Mikeladze and Kiknadze (1966) and Kiknadze (1968), on the efferent connections of the proreal gyrus both with the neocortex and with subcortical structures (Figs. 3 and 4). These authors removed a part of the proreal gyrus in dogs (field F_2 of Adrianov and Mering, 1959) and traced the efferent pathways by the method of degeneration of nerve fibers (by the Zambrzhitskii modification of Nauta's method). Observations of the course and termination of degenerated nerve fibers showed that the proreal gyrus sends efferents to many cortical fields. Especially close connections were noted with fields distributed in direct proximity to the portion of the cortex that had been removed. These, in the first instance, were the rostral portion of the proreal gyrus, the anterior and posterior cruciate gyri, the orbital gyrus, and finally the middle part of the lateral gyrus (*Sga*, *Sgp*, *Or*, and *Lm* in Fig. 3). In these parts of the cortex, degenerating fibers were rather numerous. The largest portion was distributed in layers IV and III, and a smaller portion appeared in layer II and extended to the first layer.

In fields at a greater distance from the proreal gyrus (i.e., the fields of the visual analyzer, the sylvian gyrus, etc.), the quantity of degenerating fibers is sharply diminished. In these regions of the cortex, the degenerated fibers reached only the lower layers of the cortex (V and VI).

For study of the extensive connections of the proreal gyrus with the

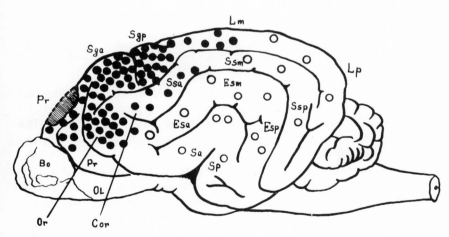

Fig. 3. Cortical efferent connections of the proreal gyrus of the dog. The portion of the proreal gyrus removed is shown striped (Pr). Filled circles denote portions of the cortex receiving the largest number of nerve fibers from the proreal gyrus, the density of the circles corresponding to the intensity of the degeneration of fibers. Open circles denote locations of the least degeneration of fibers, in particular, those reaching layers V and VI. Sga—g. sigmoideus ant.; Sgp—g. sigmoideus post.; Esa—g. ectosylv. ant.; Esm—g. ectosylv. med.; Esp—g. ectosylv. post.; Sa— g. suprasylv. ant.; Sp—g. sylv. post.; Or—g. orbitalis; Cor—g. coronaris; Lm—g. lateralis med.; Lp—g. lateralis post (Mikeladze and Kiknadze).

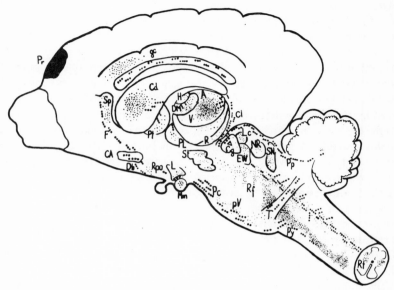

Fig. 4. Efferent connections of the proreal gyrus of the cortex with the old (archipaleo) cortex and subcortical structures of the brain in the cat and dog. The short chains denote pathways, and the small dots denote terminations of degenerating nerve fibers. gc—cingulate gyrus; Cd—caudate nucleus; Pt—putamen; PL—globus pallidus; Sp—septum pellucidum; CA—anterior commissure; f—fornix; Db—diagonal band; H—frenulum; A—anterior nucleus of the thalamus; DM—dorsomedial nucleus of the thalamus; R—reticular nucleus of the thalamus; ci—internal capsule; sth—subthalamic region; L—lateral hypothalamus; Rpo—supraoptic region; Mm—mammillary bodies; Pc—cerebral peduncles; Lc—locus ceruleus; EW—Edinger–Westphal nucleus; NR—red nucleus; SN—substantia nigra; Pp—cerebellar peduncles; Rf—reticular substance; pV—pons; T—trapezoid body; Py—pyramids; Rt—spinal reticular substance (Mikeladze and Kiknadze, 1966).

archipaleocortex and with subcortical structures, Mikeladze and Kiknadze (1966) removed the entire proreal gyrus of one hemisphere in cats, but in dogs, as was mentioned above, only a part of the gyrus was removed. The results of the studies by these authors are shown in Fig. 4, the degenerations they found being represented by the areas of stippling.

As is obvious from Fig. 4, the proreal gyrus in the dog and cat is connected with many subcortical structures. A large mass of degenerating fibers course along the internal capsule; thence a portion of them turn to the *caudate nucleus* and also to the *putamen* and *globus pallidus*. At this level, the degenerated fibers were also found in the *fornix, septum pellucidum*, and in the *anterior commissure*. From the internal capsule the degenerated fibers extended to the dorsomedial and ventral nuclei of the thalamus. Fibers were found in the reticular nucleus of the thalamus, but they passed through this nucleus without terminating, whereas in the first two nuclei, fibers were distributed on the body of neurons. Removal of the proreal gyrus also resulted in degeneration of fibers in the hypothalamic and subthalamic regions, less so in the substantia nigra and in cells of the red nucleus. The proreal gyrus is connected also with the intrinsic nuclei of the pons, and with the trapezoid body. Degeneration of fibers was found in the middle cerebellar peduncle and in the cerebellar cortex, although the cerebellum was not studied in detail. Numerous degenerations were noted among cells of the reticular formation, predominantly in the lateral part of the midbrain and medulla. Lesser, but rather clear degeneration was traced along the pyramids and in the reticular substance of the spinal gray matter. Kiknadze and Mikeladze (1968) also investigated the afferent innervation of the proreal gyrus from different parts of the cortex and from subcortical structures. The results of these experiments are depicted in Fig. 5, in which it is evident that the proreal gyrus is connected not only with the immediately adjacent orbital gyrus, but also with the sigmoid gyrus, to a lesser degree with the sylvian and ectosylvian gyri of the neocortex, with the cingulate gyrus and the archipaleocortex, and also with the sub- and hypothalamic regions, and the substantia nigra.

Oscillographic study of the proreal gyrus upon stimulation of sensory organs clearly shows that it responds electrically to stimulation of all re-

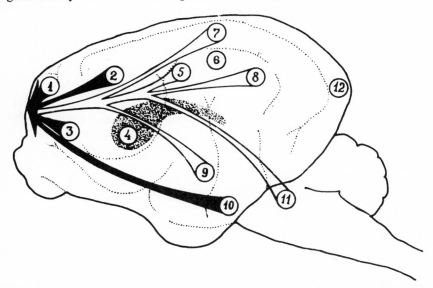

Fig. 5. Afferent connections of the proreal gyrus in the cat. The numbered circles denote the portions of the cortex removed. 1—anterior sigmoid gyrus; 2—anterior part of the cingulate gyrus; 3—orbital gyrus; 4—caudate nucleus; 5—anterior portion of the medial ectosylvian gyrus; 6—middle portion of the cingulate gyrus; 7—middle portion of the suprasylvian gyrus; 8—posterior portion of the middle ectosylvian gyrus; 9—anterior sylvian gyrus; 10—subthalamic and posterior hypothalamic regions; 11—substantia nigra; Pr—proreal gyrus; 12—visual cortex (Mikeladze and Kiknadze, 1968).

I   II   III   IV

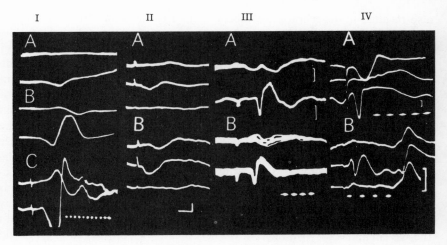

Fig. 6. I and II. Responses of the proreal gyrus and the somatosensory cortex to cutaneous stimulation of the anterior extremity and the tongue. Bipolar recordings in chloralose preparations. Stimuli are single electrical discharges. I. Responses of the proreal (upper trace) and somatosensory (lower trace) gyri. Intensity of stimuli: A, 0.5 V; B, 1 V; C, 10 V. II. Responses from the proreal gyrus (upper trace), orbital cortex (middle trace), and medial suprasylvian gyrus (lower trace). Intensity of stimuli: A, 2.1 V; B, 2.7 V. III. Response of the proreal gyrus and visual area to flashes of light. Bipolar recording. Responses from the proreal gyri (upper trace) and visual projection area (lower trace). A—in response to a single flash of light; B—superposition of responses to flashes of light with a rhythm of 0.5 per sec. IV. Responses of the proreal gyrus and the visual and auditory areas to sound impulses. Chloralose preparation. Monopolar recordings. A—recording from the proreal gyrus (upper trace), visual area (middle trace), and auditory area (lower trace). B—another preparation—Proreal gyrus (upper trace), auditory (middle trace), and visual (lower trace) regions. Note that a response to the sound impulses appears only in the auditory region. Time calibration 20 msec; voltage calibration: A, 0.2 mV; B, 0.5 mV (Eristavi, 1968).

ceptors. In Fig. 6, e.g., the proreal gyrus responds to stimulation of the skin of the contralateral forepaw (I) and tongue (II), and also to light (III) and auditory (IV) stimuli. In all cases, as is evident in the figure, these responses arose in the proreal gyrus significantly later than in the corresponding projection regions of the cortex (Eristavi, 1968). This finding indicates that in all cases of stimulation of the receptors, the proreal gyrus perceived them not by direct pathways, but by intermediate centers such as the primary zones of the cortex and thalamus.

On the basis of the above-mentioned disturbances of memory for all modalities of perception following ablation of the proreal gyrus, and on the basis of the histological data concerning afferent and efferent fibers of the proreal gyrus following localized damage to the cortex, we propose that *all primary areas of the cerebral cortex are bilaterally connected by association neurons not only with secondary areas, but also with the inferior temporal lobes and with the proreal gyri. They must be excited together during each perception of the external world, and short-term memory is basically the result of conjoined activity of these cortical regions.*

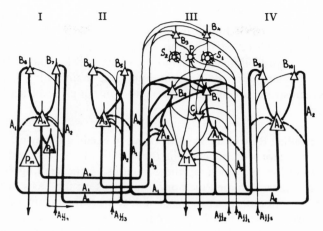

Fig. 7. Schema of neural structure of visual memory. The proreal gyrus, the secondary visual area, the primary visual area, the inferior temporal lobe, and the hippocampus are depicted in the figure. S_1 and S_2 are stellate sensory neurons; P—stellate interneuron; B_1 to B_{10}, internuncial pyramidal neurons; A_1 to A_5—association pyramidal neurons; C—stellate projection neurons of Cajal for eye movements; M—projection pyramidal neurons of Meinert of the neck during an orienting response; Aff_1 and Aff_2—afferents of the specific visual system; Aff_3, Aff_4, and Aff_5—afferents of the nonspecific system. The heavy lines denote fibers of closed neuronal circuits activated by visual perception or by a visual image. The thin lines denote unidirectional connections of neural circuits with stellate neurons producing the image, and with projection neurons of the orienting response. The dashed lines denote possible collateral connections in the closed neural circuits. The system of associational cells A_3, A_4, and A_5 are presumed to serve for retention of the visual images in memory. The reproduction of the latter upon activation of one of the parts of the object occurs in the following manner: Upon excitation of a part of the object by Aff_1, e.g., excitation in the primary area S_1, P, B_1, C, M, and A_1 begins, and the perception of this part arises and an appropriate orienting response is evoked (by C and M). Then the excitation is propagated by A_1 to the secondary area, activating B_5 and A_3, B_8 and A_4 in the proreal gyrus, and B_9 and A_5 in the temporal lobe. From A_3, A_4, and A_5 impulses return to the primary visual area and activate finally B_1 and B_2, thus resulting by these pathways in an activated condition of the entire system of neural circuits, and secondly, by B_3 and B_4, activate the system of stellate cells S_1, S_2, and P, thus reproducing the image of the entire object and evoking an appropriate orienting response. Moreover, from A_4, on the one hand, the efferent pyramidal neurons, P_m, are activated which lead to subcortical structures for evoking coordinated somatovegetative behavioral responses, and on the other hand, efferent pyramidal neurons, P_{sm}, are activated, which project to the sensorimotor region of the cortex for production of instrumental movements.

In Fig. 7, a schema is presented of the neural structure of the cortex and its neural connections that basically participate in visual perception of an object and reproduction of its visual image. If the extensive connections of the proreal gyrus with the neocortex, the archipaleocortex and subcortical structures are kept in mind, as these were given in Figs. 4 and 5, then it can be asserted that delayed responses arising on the basis of image memory must be accomplished by means of the efferent system of the proreal gyrus.

As will be evident below, the perceiving regions of the cortex are connected with the cortical parts of the archipaleocortex (such as the cingulate gyrus and the hippocampus) and also with subcortical structures (such as the caudate nucleus, the amygdala, and the cerebellum). Bilateral destruction of the latter also leads to temporary absence of image memory, but the disturbance of image memory that results must presumably be of another origin. These parts of the archi- and paleocortex and subcortical structures evidently influence memory in such a way that they act on the neocortex by means of its afferent impulses, maintaining the excitability of neural substrates of image memory to some high level necessary for its activation.

The Leading Role of the Proreal Gyrus in Feeding Behavior. The existence of different regions of memory in the cortex of the cerebral hemispheres raises a question of which of these regions is the leading one. It seems to me that since we studied memory in animals on the basis of their feeding behavior, we should speak only of a leading substratum of memory for feeding objects. There is a basis for presuming that such a substratum for retention and recall of the food object and for the execution of the corresponding behavior is found in the prefrontal region, where the primary zone of gustatory and tactile perception for the oral cavity and also the motor zone for the act of eating is located in the orbital gyrus. The proreal gyrus itself, evidently, is a secondary area for these gustatory and tactile perceptions, and it itself, evidently, is a secondary area, together with the orbital gyrus, for olfactory reception. In the proreal gyrus of cats, large pyramidal cells which are of an associational nature and characterize secondary areas are richly represented (Kaada, 1951; Mikeladze and Kiknadze, 1968).

It is known that secondary responses to cutaneous stimulation (Alikishibekova, 1965, and others), to sound, to light stimuli, and to electrical stimulation of the optic nerve (Buser and Borenstein, 1965; Alikishibekova, 1965, and others) are found in the orbital area. The proreal gyri respond with almost the same manner to the same stimuli (Eristavi, 1968). In exactly the same way, the orbital cortex responds with secondary responses to stimulation of the olfactory bulb along with the proreal gyrus (Kaada, 1951). Finally, we now know that the orbital and proreal gyri produce synchronized slow potential in the form of a recruiting response, both spontaneously and upon stimulation of cutaneous receptors (Alikishibekova, 1965).

All of the above-mentioned facts indicate that the orbital and proreal gyri function as a single unified system that becomes a primary and secondary area for single perceptual regions and here, evidently, originates the mutual integration of all of the sensory inputs and the efferent neuronal complexes related to the intake of food.

Since during each intake of food, excitation of the orbital and proreal gyri occurs by visual, auditory, cutaneous, gustatory, and olfactory stimuli of the food object, and at the same time the corresponding visual, auditory, cutaneous, gustatory, and olfactory perceptual areas are excited, then among all of these excited regions of the cortex closed neuronal circuits are readily established. Moreover, in the association neurons of the proreal gyri which participate in these circuits, the above-mentioned formation of persistent active protein in the postsynaptic regions of cells evidently occurs profusely, even upon the first activation of these circuits. Thus they can effect the reproduction of the image of food and its location for a long period and at the same time effect the appropriate delayed response of feeding movements. To such an explanation attests, in the first place, the fact that following bilateral ablation of the proreal gyrus, delayed feeding movement responses for all aspects of perception of the food object are impaired for a long time, and do not become fully restored.

It is also true, however, that memory of a feeding object is impaired by bilateral damage to the temporal lobes and to the hippocampus, in such a way that it is impaired temporarily both for the perception by individual sense organs as well as for complex perception of the food object. Memory is also impaired by bilateral damage of the secondary areas of perceiving regions. In this case, with injury to each of these areas, memory is affected only for perception of the corresponding modality. Therefore, it can be presumed that all of these parts of the new and old cortex normally constitute a single, integral formation, and since stable active protein is formed in the association neurons of all of these parts, they must all participate in the establishment and retention of the image of the external world. Upon exclusion of one of the links, the remaining ones do not lose their functional role. Since each link is connected by means of bilateral connections with all remaining ones as well as with the primary areas, the entire system must therefore be capable of being activated by any primary area which perceives part of the given object or its surroundings. As a result of this reciprocally related activity, the function of intact links can be sufficient for activation of pyramidal and extrapyramidal pathways to the coordinating mechanisms of the somatovegetative response that are operative in producing the feeding behavior.

If it is kept in mind that the proreal gyri are widely connected with the premotor and sensorimotor regions of the cortex, as well as with all of the principal somatosensory coordinating mechanisms of subcortical formations, then it can be asserted that upon activation of the entire unified system of the substrates of memory, the external responses are evoked in the main by the proreal gyri.

It must be presumed that instrumental movements of the extremities and in general localized coordinating movements of the organism ensue as a result of the premotor and sensorimotor gyri, and that all somatovegetative responses of an emotional character, and also such responses as are common for all behavior such as locomotion, pricking up the ears, orienting movement of the head, etc., ensue from corticofugal pathways of the proreal gyrus.

Moreover, if it is kept in mind that prolonged retention of the perceived object is a basic condition of mental activity, and that the latter depends in a major way on association neurons of the proreal gyri, then it can also be asserted that intellectual phylogenetic development of vertebrates originates basically as a result of a quantitative growth and qualitative development of the association neurons of the proreal gyrus.

Thus, among the complex of cortical parts of short-term memory that participate in the retention of the image of food and its location, as well as in the elicitation of delayed responses, the proreal gyri constitute a major link. Since all of these cortical links of short-term memory are connected bilaterally, the removal of one of them, the proreal gyri in particular, does not lead to complete loss of memory but only to a more or less significant impairment of it.

Data from the Literature Concerning the Origin of Short-Term Memory. The explanation of the phenomenon of memory which makes use of the idea of reverberating circuits has been advanced by many authors (Lashley, 1950; Hebb, 1961, and others), but the most detailed development of this concept has been made by Konorski. Beginning from approximately the same facts concerning short-term memory as we have already mentioned, as manifested in the visual perception of the placing of a basin with food behind one of the screens standing at a short distance in front of the animal, he explains short-term memory in the following manner: He finds that, in general, this memory is dependent on traces of excitation that have remained in closed neural circuits of association neurons, in which the excitation can circulate for some time after cessation of stimulation, and that the duration of the interval is determined by the strength of these traces. At the same time he proposes that the principal factor determining the delayed behavior of the animal is the localization of food at the time that it had been shown beforehand. Since during the delay period, the orientation of the animal's body can be very different (e.g., the animal can even be taken out of the experimental room in this period), then it must be concluded, Konorski states, that this memory, usually termed by him as recent memory, is based purely on intercentral neural processes occurring in the brain during the delay period. These processes, according to Konorski, determine the direction of feeding behavior in space, which the animal recalls during the delay period under the influence of proprioceptive or labyrinthine stimuli, or both.

Comparing these arguments of Konorski with our conception of image psychoneural behavior, it can be concluded that the intercentral processes which according to Konorski determine the direction of feeding behavior are just the same, in our opinion, as those various psychoneural processes which reproduce the image of the food and its location. But in this process, the recalled direction of behavior is determined, not by the proprioceptive and labyrinthine stimuli occurring at the given moment, as Konorski says, but by the reproduction of psychoneural processes of the visual–auditory or vestibular spatial image of the direction to the location of food.

Experiments have also been carried out to clarify the delayed response in relation to the teachings of Pavlov on higher nervous activity. Thus Shustin (1959) examined delayed responses by the following method: In one series, three pans with covers were placed in front of the eyes of the dog at a distance of 0.7 m. Meat was then placed in one of these within the view of the animal, after which all three pans were covered. The food placed in the pan thus acted simultaneously on visual, auditory, and olfactory receptors. After various intervals of time, the dog, which had been kept behind the screen, was allowed to go to the pans.

In the overwhelming majority of cases, intact dogs responded appropriately. They immediately opened the pan that had been filled with food, and did not open the empty ones. The maximum delay for the appropriate response was 3 min.

Shustin found that this occurred in response to the traces of the complex of stimuli which had been retained during the delay interval, as occurs during trace-conditioned reflexes. He states: "This function of retention of the traces of the complex of stimuli that are important for the animal can be carried out correctly from our point of view as the result of concentration of excitation and inhibition in the cerebral hemispheres" (1959, p. 98). This concentration is such that it occurs with three phases: "excitation, inhibition, and excitation." The first excitation is the result of the effect of the natural food stimuli at a distance, and the second excitation results from the arrival of the moment of reinforcement with food (1961, p. 95). This conditioned reflex explanation, which is actually not an explanation but rather a statement of the character of the external response, Shustin assumes to be just the same as that for the delayed response, which was studied by Jacobson, Konorski, Voitonis, and others, who worked with other methods and established a maximum delay of up to 10 to 12 min.

It should further be noted that in the experiments of Shustin, the food was given predominantly in the same corner of the feeder and a conditioned trace reflex to the place of food was of course elaborated in the dog, as Shustin himself noted. Therefore, his entire theoretical consideration concerned the elaboration of trace-conditioned reflexes, and not the delayed response which was studied by us, Konorski, and others, in which delayed responses after the very first perception of a new location of food was observed.

It is characteristic that this conditioned reflex to a specific basin was not disturbed if in the subsequent pause, the dog went off to the side or became somnolent. Frequently, the dog initially approached an empty feeder or one from which it had eaten in the preceding trial following sufficient consolidation of the trace movement reflex. These observations indicate that under the conditions of formation of trace-conditioned reflexes, the behavior of the animal is also regulated to a significant degree by the image of the location of food.

ORIGIN OF LONG-TERM IMAGE MEMORY

As was indicated previously, we have observed long-term memory for the location of food that is apparent for many days after its perception, only if the animal had been brought to the place of food so that it could eat or smell the latter. We have already stated that the possibility of reproduction of the image of the location of food after several hours, days, or even months following a single perception cannot be based on a set of structural or functional changes of association neuronal circuits of the cortex; rather, more or less prolonged retention of the image of the food object must be based on molecular and submolecular changes in the cytoplasm of cells, first of all in the postsynaptic regions of the association pyramidal neurons. These changes must be determined by the synthesis of a special protein that participates in the plastic changes of the postsynaptic membrane.

The Hypothesis of Hydén on the Origin of Long-Term Memory. We should now consider the manner of formation of this active protein, and its role in the retention and recall of the image of the object perceived. The most fully elaborated hypothesis is that of Hydén (1960). He presumes that upon perception of an object, a multiple self-excitation of chains of neural circuits occurs which is accompanied by the occurrence of distinctive electrical discharges having characteristic modulation frequencies, and which result in specific changes in the ionic equilibrium in the cytoplasm of the excited nerve cells. Among these electrical discharges must be included localized postsynaptic potentials, the number and distribution of which in the body of the cell are entirely determined by the number and distribution of the excited synaptic endings. It must further be kept in mind that with each peripheral impulse from the receptor, these endings are not excited simultaneously but with very different latent periods, and such activation is repeated during each cycle of excitation in the neural circuit. Thus it is entirely natural that during perception of each object, local processes must arise in nerve cells that have specific frequency characteristic and modulation. Hydén supposes that ionic equilibrium in the cytoplasm of the cell changes differently, depending on the characteristic features of the object perceived, i.e., depending on the frequency characteristic and modulation of the electrical discharges. This particular change of ionic equilibrium in the cytoplasm, in Hydén's opinion, has a particular effect on the nucleus of the nerve cell, as the result of which the ribonucleic acid (RNA) is formed with a characteristic change of composition of its base. This specific RNA results in the formation of the particular protein in the cytoplasm of the nerve cells. This means, according to Hydén, that upon perception of each external object, a specific protein corresponding to it is formed, which must then function as a regulator of the action of the mediator determining the conduction of impulses across synapses. Hydén, as well as Schmitt (1962), assumes that this specific protein is formed anew upon the inflow of the next frequency-modulated signal identical with that which "initiated" the original process of formation of the specific protein macromolecule. If this macromolecule is produced in the process of metabolism and establishes the condition for reproduction of the information received earlier, then the latter phenomenon presumably originates as a result of the fact that the macromolecules are capable of self-renewal each time that the corresponding "command" for this is received.

The perception of the food object originates in a specific situation. Consequently, the excitation of neuronal circuits by a food object must occur in connection with those circuits that are excited by the situation, especially by that part of it which occurs in direct proximity to the given object. Under our conditions, trials in this situation entail not only the location of the food, but also the entire situation in the experimental room, including the experimenter, the attendant personnel, and also the stairs and corridor along which we led the dog from the vivarium. It must be the combined effect of the food object and the situation directly surrounding the particular object which produces, in the complex chain of activated neuronal circuits of the cortex, those electrical discharges with specific modulation of frequencies which, according to Hydén, evoke specific reconstitution of RNA with formation of a specific protein–activator in the cytoplasm of the given neuronal circuits. This reconstitution of RNA and the formation of the specific protein must occur on the first occasion and is retained for a long time.

Discussion of the Hypothesis of Hydén. Hydén's hypothesis is contradicted by certain facts. It is impossible, for example, to imagine that repeated excitation of neural circuits occurs only as a result of activation of a specific protein which had been formed in the neural circuits upon the first excitation, and that only a specific modulation of frequencies of electrical discharges constitute the condition of activation of this specific protein, and thus the neural circuits of the given image. According to contemporary neurophysiology, excitation of a cell and its axon originates under the influence of electrical currents evoked by localized postsynaptic potentials. If the first time the excitation of pyramidal cells *via* given neural terminations occurs without participation of the specific RNA and the specific protein produced by it, then the repeated excitation must also occur in the same way. Moreover we know that the activation of neuronal circuits of a given image occurs not only from repetition of the effect of the given object, but even of only a part of it, or if the surrounding environment is repeated, and thus the modulation of electrical discharges in the associational neural cells of the given circuit must be very different.

Presumably, the significance of the active protein formed during the first perception of the object must be important because it is concentrated in the synaptic endings of cells, and thus continues to act on the postsynaptic membrane so as to strengthen and prolong localized transsynaptic potentials occurring upon excitation of presynaptic neural endings. Accordingly, the activation of the axonal hillock is of course increased and prolonged; as a result of this, the axon can react by a series of spreading discharges,

Further, as is known, at the time of excitation, RNA appears in the cytoplasm of the cell, which is formed initially in the nucleus. It accumulates and is retained, primarily under the cellular membrane in the postsynaptic regions (Morrell, 1961, and others), for a time of greater or lesser extent. Moreover, we presume that the quantity of ribosomes, which also contain ribonucleic acid (D'yachkova and Manteifel', 1969), also increases during excitation. It must be presumed that with each perception of the external object this and other types of RNA, mutually interacting with proteins and phospholipids, synthesize a particular type of active protein. The latter, acting on the postsynaptic membrane, produces in it a specific plastic change which results in an increased conductivity of excitation. This protein, after formation, is retained for some time and upon each new effect of the given object, the quantity of it increases and consequently its facilitating action on the cell is increased and prolonged. Moreover, it is quite possible that this protein–activator is resynthesized after metabolic destruction. It must further be assumed that the accumulation of the active protein is localized, in the cell, to those postsynaptic regions on which the neural terminations of the excited neural circuits were acting. Only under this condition can the accumulation of such an active protein play a specific role in the activation of the given neural circuit. Also, the fact that the stronger and the longer the external influence, the longer the memory of it is retained appears to confirm the deduction that it is not a question of the specificity of a protein characteristic for the perception of each object; rather, the quantitative increase of the protein-activator and its stability must play an important role in the retention of the traces of the effect of the external world.

Against the specificity of proteins formed from participation of a genetic mechanism (DNA–RNA), the following should also be mentioned: The modulation of the frequencies of the electrical discharges must be very different in different pyramidal cells which are activated from perception of a single object, depending on the different number and different distribution of synaptic endings, and the different sequences of their excitation. Thus, a disturbance of the ionic equilibrium in different nerve cells of a given neural circuit would occur differently. If one adheres to the hypothesis of Hydén, its influence on DNA must correspondingly be different and will lead to the formation of a different specific RNA and a different specific protein in these nerve cells.

It would be more plausible to presume that electrical discharges of a given modulation of frequencies that alter the ionic equilibrium lead to activation of RNA–intermediaries and ribosomal RNA, which in turn stimulates the formation of a particular type of active protein. The latter protein, concentrating in the excited postsynaptic regions, continuously acts as an activator on the postsynaptic membrane. In this way, the given protein facilitates the transmission of excitation, on the one hand, and on the other, strengthens the localized postsynaptic potentials. Since the potentials arising in different postsynaptic regions form currents which combine to reach different amplitudes and durations, then under their influence the axon can be excited not only once, but many times in response to a single afferent impulse. Such a result is actually observed in unit recordings of excited cells in the central nervous system.

Kometiani and Aleksidze (1967) maintain the view that the retention and reproduction of information in nerve cells cannot be reduced either to specific proteins or to other particular compounds of some kind. The system of DNA–RNA protein in a nerve cell, just as in all other cells, is accomplished by the genetic memory which is related to the reproduction of inherited characteristics. However, memory itself, which is a function of the brain, is not inherited. A leading role in such memory must be played by those intercellular interrelationships that are specific for nerve tissue, but not for any other. It must be taken for granted that the functional activity of nerve tissues in the first instance finds its expression in the processes of membranes, i.e., in electrical activity, and in the effect of mediators and enzymatic transformations. These processes are accompanied by structural changes of membranes, breakdown, and rapid restoration. For the formation of membranes and for the restoration of their enzymes and the regulators of metabolism, an increase in synthesis of proteins is necessary. Thus, as a result of such complex processes, an active protein is synthesized which effects an increased readiness of synaptic membranes for transmission of excitation.

It thus follows that the assumption of the retention and reproduction of information in the brain is effected by complex dynamic processes in which the system of DNA–RNA, active protein, membrane structures, mediators, enzymes, and regulators of metabolic transmissions assume a direct part.

But for perception of a specific object and then for its retention in the form of an image that is projected into the surrounding external medium, it is necessary that these molecular and submolecular processes occur in all those very complex composites of pyramidal neurons that participated in the perception of the given object. Because of these processes, then, all of these neurons become connected with one another in a more or less stable manner, so as to form a single integrated functional system.

Thus, in each activated association pyramidal cell, an RNA–intermediary and active protein must arise, but these are not specific for perception of each new object as Hydén supposes. One and the same active protein is formed with absolutely identical characteristics. However, the latter can be of different concentrations and differently distributed within the cell, depending on the location of the activated postsynaptic regions. This activated protein basically serves for establishment of stable long-term connections between all association pyramidal neurons activated by the given object.

The Reproduction of the Image of the Location of Food upon Perception of a Part of the Object, or a Part of Its Environment. The above described conjecture of the origin of long-term image memory can be satisfactory for the reproduction of the image upon repetition of the perception of the entire object. But the reproduction of the image of a given object can also occur upon perception of only a part of the object or a part of the surroundings. For understanding of this phenomenon it must be assumed that internuncial and association pyramidal neurons that are excited upon perception of the given object also have innate connections among themselves, i.e., the axon of each cell is connected with other cells by means of collaterals. Thus, pyramidal cells which are primarily excited upon perception of the given object and its environment must secondarily be excited by collaterals from axons of those primarily excited cells. It must be kept in mind that the primary excitation of pyramidal cells originates across one synapse and the above-mentioned active protein is formed in their postsynaptic regions, at the same time that a disturbance of ionic equilibrium must also influence all of the remaining postsynaptic regions, thus changing their permeability in some measure and facilitating the excitation of them. This has been shown by physiological experiments. Upon stimulating two parts of the cerebral cortex, it can be observed that the stimulation of one part facilitates the effect on the other part. This phenomenon can be explained only by assuming a convergence of excited axons from different parts of the cerebral cortex on the same nerve cells. The same is observed upon stimulation of receptive fields of a spinal reflex: stimulation of one part of the skin strongly facilitates the effect of stimulation of another part. Such facilitatory effect can originate only if there are nerve cells in the spinal cord that are common to these two parts of the receptive field.

Thus, it is clear that the pyramidal cells that are excited primarily can excite secondarily, by their axons and collaterals, all those other cells in which the ionic permeability of synaptic membranes had been increased by the primary excitation. Localized potentials from the secondarily excited postsynaptic portions in turn can also activate the nuclear substance, and the resulting RNA intermediary is then transferred to the secondarily excited postsynaptic regions, where active protein can also originate.

It thus follows that, with the activation of neural circuits upon perception of a given object, stable, active protein arises not only in the primarily excited postsynaptic regions, but also in secondarily excited regions. Owing to this process, when the effect of a part of the object or of its circumstances occurs, the entire complex of a neural circuit excited by perception of the object can be excited, i.e., a part of the object or of its environment excites primarily a small part of the nerve cells of the given complex of neural circuits, but their axons and collaterals excite the remaining cells of the given circuit. As a result, the entire image of the given object is reproduced.

The Pathways of Activation of Sensory Neurons and of Projection Pyramids. It is reasonable to assume that, in the formation of closed neural circuits, the projection pyramidal neurons of the cortex that result in orienting responses (e.g., the cells of Meinert and Cajal), or in defensive and instrumental movement of the extremities, do not participate directly. Sensory neurons with a terminal axonal net and which do not have axonal connections with pyramidal cells (cell S_1 in Figs. 8 and 9) also probably do not participate in these closed neural circuits. The latter must then be constituted, in the main, of internuncial and association pyramidal neurons. In the perceiving regions, certain stellate cells with axons recurrent to pyramidal cells (cells S_2, P, and P_1 in Figs. 8 and 9) may also be included. Pyramidal neurons of the neuronal circuits are connected *via* their own collaterals directly and *via* internuncial neurons, with projection pyramids and stellate sensory neurons (cells M and S_1 in Figs. 8 and 9) (Beritashvili, 1961). Therefore, it must be supposed that excitation that is distributed along an association neuronal circuit activates both sensory and projectional neurons more or less simultaneously (Figs. 8 and 9).

On the basis of histological data, it is also known that these neural circuits consisting of association and internuncial pyramidal cells are unilaterally connected with projection pyramids and stellate sensory neurons. Therefore, the latter cells are excited each time the given neural circuit

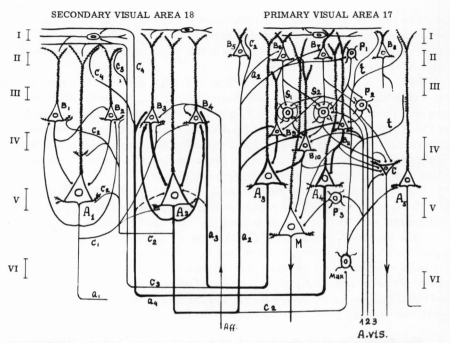

SECONDARY VISUAL AREA 18   PRIMARY VISUAL AREA 17

Fig. 8. Schema of neuronal circuits of the visual region which produce visual perception in man and the orienting response. S_1 and S_2—stellate sensory neurons; P_1, P_2, and P_3—internuncial stellate neurons; B_1 to B_{11}—internuncial pyramidal neurons; A_1 to A_5—association neurons; M—pyramidal projection neuron of Meinert; C—projection oculomotor neurons, stellate cells of Cajal; Mar—internuncial neuron of Martinotti; a_1 to a_4—axons of association neurons; c_3 and c_4—their collaterals. In the primary zone of the visual cortex, afferent visual fibers (A. vis.) from the thalamus terminate on stellate and internuncial neurons of layer IV, and also on the cell of the oculomotor neuron. These stellate and internuncial neurons are connected with cell of association neurons (A_3 and A_4) and with cells of Meinert. The latter cells are also connected with thalamic fibers by stellate cell P_3. This system of neurons, upon excitation of the lateral geniculate fibers, results on the one hand in perception of the object, and on the other, in an orienting response of the head and eyes, with the result of fixation on the particular object.

Axons from association neurons A_3 and A_4 cross over to the secondary visual area and there terminate on the cell bodies of internuncial neurons B_3 and B_4, the axons of which converge on the association cell A_2. The axon of the latter cell projects to the primary visual area and there terminates on cells of internuncial neurons of layer IV (B_9, B_{10}, and B_{11}). Closed neuronal circuits, which are denoted by heavy lines, are thus established. These circuits are activated not only by simultaneous excitation of all three visual pathways (1, 2, and 3), but also by each of them separately. Association fibers from the secondary area also terminate on internuncial pyramidal and stellate cells of layer II, which in turn are connected with stellate sensory cells. Upon visual perception, all of these neural connections are also activated and thus a functionally connected system is established which persists for a greater or lesser interval of time and serves for reproduction of the image of the entire object, upon being acted upon visually by only a part of it. The collateral C_2 of the axon of the association neuron A_2 terminates on the internuncial cell Mar in the primary area, the axon of which is in contact with dendrites in the upper layers. In just the same way, axons of association neurons A_3 and A_4, extending into the secondary area, give off collaterals C_3 and C_4 which terminate mainly on dendrites of the upper layers. By means of these collaterals, activation of the dendrites of the neighboring internuncial and association neurons occurs, resulting in generalized inhibition of them, thus permitting excitation in the given functional system to be localized. Connections of nonspecific thalamic fibers, Aff, with the secondary visual zone are also shown in the schema.

is excited. Sensory neurons of higher phylogenetic development that have a pericellular axonal network and projectional pyramidal neurons do not send axons to association pyramidal neurons. Therefore, they cannot participate in the formation of neural circuits of the cortex (Beritashvili, 1961).

We have already indicated that in the formation of a given neuronal circuit each nerve cell participates not as a whole, but only with those

AUDITORY CORTEX   ASSOCIATION AREA   VISUAL CORTEX

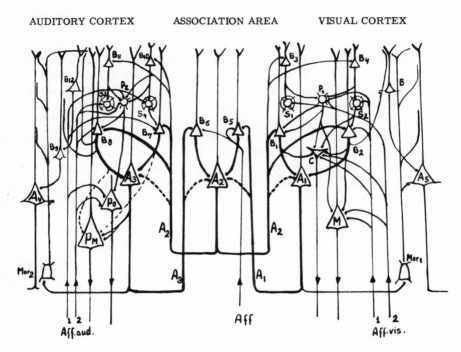

Fig. 9. Schema of neural circuits connecting the auditory and the visual perceiving regions of the cortex, for perception and for establishing the image of an auditory object. The letters denote the same structures as in the preceding figure. Upon stimulation by a particular object, thalamic fibers Aff and Aff_{vis}, in the corresponding perceiving cortical regions activate stellate sensory neurons (S_1 to S_4) of layer IV and also internuncial neurons (B_1, B_2, B_7, and B_8). Association neurons A_1 and A_3 are activated by these neurons, the axons of which project to the association field and converge on internuncial neurons B_5 and B_6. The latter activate cells of association neuron A_2, from which axons pass into the auditory and visual perceiving regions and there terminate on internuncial neurons of layer IV. Thus, closed circuits are denoted by heavy lines formed between the auditory and visual areas.

From the association neurons of these layers, collaterals rise to layer II, exciting internuncial neurons therein. By the latter, both sensory neurons (S_1 to S_4) and projecting neurons of Meinert (M) and Cajal (C) are also excited. The activation of this entire system of neurons results in perception and establishment of a visual–auditory image of the given object. This functional system is retained for a more or less prolonged interval of time. According to this scheme, upon stimulation by some part of the object (in the schema, the corresponding afferent given the numbers 1, 2 Aff_{aud} and 1, 2 Aff_{vis}; nonspecific afferent pathways to the association regions are denoted by Aff), the entire system of neurons is excited, with reproduction of the entire image of the object perceived and appearance of the corresponding orienting response of the head.

specific postsynaptic regions in which localized processes arise from excitation of the given neural circuit. From this it follows that an association pyramidal cell can participate in neural circuits of different perceptions, owing to participation of different synaptic parts of the cell.

As has been indicated above, excitation from given associational neural circuits crosses over *via* unidirectional connections to stellate sensory neurons, thus producing the image of the object perceived, and to efferent projection neurons, producing the orienting response. But excitation from the intermediary and association neuronal circuits activated by the given perception do not cross over to other association pyramidal neurons and do not excite other neural circuits. This occurs because all of these neurons must undergo a generalized inhibition which is evoked as a result of activation of their apical and basal dendrites *via* collaterals of activated intermediary and association neurons (see Figs. 8 and 9), since this always occurs with excitation of any neuronal circuit in the cerebral cortex (Beritashvili, 1961, 1963). But this general inhibition must also originate from the reticular formation which is activated by corticofugal pathways from the association neuronal circuits of the cortex that are activated by the given object. All of this, incidentally, determines the localization of the given image, and also the impossibility of simultaneous generation of several images by excitation from different objects.

In Fig. 8, a schematic representation is given of the neuronal structure of the visual image, and in Fig. 9, of the visual–auditory area.

Thus, in our opinion, *those sensory neurons with pericellular axonal networks that perceive the afferent impulses under the infiuence of the external world, and produce the subjective experience of it (perception and image) do not participate in the formation of neural circuits. These sensory neurons are excited by collaterals of the neuronal circuits either directly or via inter-nuncial pyramidal neurons and transmitting stellate neurons. The projection pyramidal neurons also do not enter into these association neuronal circuits; they also are excited by collaterals of the association neurons either directly or via internuncial pyramidal neurons.*

The Role of Emotional Excitation in Short-Term and Long-Term Memory. It is characteristic that in cats and dogs memory for a place of food after visual or auditory perception alone is usually not carried over to the next day. Evidently, under the influence of only visual or auditory perception of the food object, when the dog does not see the exact location of the food and does not smell the food, it perceives only the direction toward the food. But then the active protein is not formed in such quantity and with such stability that it is retained for a long time and can effect the reproduction of the image upon repetition of the influence of the given stimulation after a day or more. One must presume that only the complex perception of the place of food, entailing smelling or eating it, can produce such intense formation of stable protein-activator that the image can be retained over the course of many days and weeks.

We suppose that the basis for the duration of retention of perceived objects depends on the degree of emotional excitation which arises during the perception. It is clear that emotional excitation arises also during a single visual or auditory perception of food, but when the perception occurs at the moment of smelling and eating of the food, it is somewhat stronger. It can be supposed that the neural and hormonal influences on the neocortex that are accompanied by emotional excitation appearing upon the perception of complex stimuli are significantly stronger than with visual or auditory perception of food alone. Accordingly, in the association pyramidal cells excited during complex perception, a considerably greater quantity of RNA-intermediary and a considerably greater quantity of active protein appears, which is of a considerably more stable form than occurs with visual perception alone.

It is probable that the difference we have established between the duration of retention of visual and auditory images can be explained in that during visual perception emotional excitation is stronger than during auditory excitation.

Thus, the degree of emotional excitation during feeding plays an essential role in relation to the duration of both short-term and long-term image-memory. With the increased emotional effect that results from neural and hormonal influences from the old cortex on the new, the functional state of the neuronal elements on the latter is improved. As a result of this activity, the duration of circulation of excitation in neuronal circuits is increased, and correspondingly the period of heightened excitability is also increased. Consequently, the duration of short-term memory must also be increased, owing to the reinforcement of emotional excitation.

Long-term image memory measured in terms of days and weeks, as has been indicated above, must depend on the quantity and stability of active protein which is formed during perception in the postsynaptic parts of the excited neuron. The formation of this protein-activator in turn then must depend on the degree of emotional excitation related to feeding, since the stronger and longer the reverberation of excitation in the neuronal circuits occurring in connection with the heightened emotional excitation, the more active protein is formed. This means that *the stronger the emotional excitation during this perception, and the greater the quantity of stable active protein formed in the postsynaptic portion, the longer the image of the perceived object is retained, and the later it can be reproduced.*

This does not mean that, in general, comparatively long-term recall of the location of the food cannot occur if it is perceived without emotional stimulation. If for several days a dog is first satiated outside the experimental room, then is led into it and in response to a specific sound begins to carry out conditioned approach behavior toward a particular feeder from which it had never previously been fed, then the following takes place: Upon leading the dog from the cage to the feeder as the given sound is presented, it does not eat the food, and turns away from it. When the procedure is repeated, the animal resists and draws back to the cage. Despite repetition of this procedure a dozen times, the dog does not elaborate a conditioned reflex of feeding behavior to the particular sound. Even under fasting conditions, this sound is not perceived by the dog as a signal for feeding behavior, but does become a signal for a defensive negative response, e.g., while sitting in the cage, the animal draws back. However, if freedom of movement is allowed under fasting conditions in the absence of the sound, the dog goes directly to that feeder from which it had seen and smelled food many times. This means that upon perception of the location of food, without emotional feeding stimulation, the image of this place of food is retained for a long time.

It is characteristic that only the view and odor of food situated in a specific new place has such a very strong effect on memory, even when the animal does not experience any kind of satisfaction from it. In dogs (Aivazashvili, 1963), and in cats (Kvirtskhaliya, 1967), it was observed that if a completely oversatiated animal is shown food in an entirely new location in the room, it smells the food although it does not eat. If this same animal is led to the door of the same room on another day or even after several days under fasting conditions, in the majority of cases it goes directly to the place of food, even if the latter is taken away immediately after the animal sniffs it. This means that simply viewing and sniffing food, without accompanying emotional stimulation by the food, plays a most essential role in the establishment and retention of an enduring image of the location of food.

From this it follows that the formation of the active protein is determined also by a single visual and olfactory perception of food in the absence of an emotional stimulus of feeding. It is also established that a more significant role is played by olfaction in such combined perception. If a piece of meat in a basin is placed on a board under a glass cover which is sealed on the board with vaseline so that the animal cannot sense the odor, then after the food is shown under these conditions, the majority of animals do not go to the location of food on the next day, whereas after several hours on the same day, they do. This means that *the olfactory component is of especially great significance in the formation of the RNA-intermediary and of the active protein upon complex perception of the location of food.*

The Relation between Short-Term and Long-Term Memory. As was pointed out previously, the reproduction of the image of the perceived object originates by means of different pathways. Immediately after perception, the reproduction of the image of the external object originates from circulation of excitation in the association neuronal circuits that were activated by the perception. But the activity of these circuits cannot persist for more than some tens of seconds; more frequently, the retention is of the order of several seconds. This can take place in the absence of any kind of novelty in the surroundings immediately following the given perception. But if the perception changes, the activity of the given neural circuits will be inhibited under the influence of activity of other neural circuits from the new perceptions. Consequently, the image that is determined by activity of one neural circuit disappears with inhibition of the latter, and a new image arises in connection with activity of other neural circuits. Therefore, short-term memory, which depends on circulating excitation in neural circuits, can persist only for seconds. Beyond that, as was pointed out above, short-term memory for a given object will depend, for an additional time, on an increased excitability within these neural circuits resulting from the influence of a presynaptic mediator and from the facilitating influence of an active protein in the postsynaptic portions, from which the image of the object or the external world can be reproduced.

However, if there is strong emotional food stimulation in relation to the perception of food in the new place, the maximum delay of the appropriate behavior can be appreciably diminished if the animal has a concurrent image. For example, if the animal has eaten food in several places in a given room, then images of the location of the food in all of these places are formed by the animal. Therefore, following the last occasion of eating in one of these places, the animal may go to another feeding place which had been perceived still earlier.

Orienting behavior with respect to an image of the place of food is very strongly disturbed if, as indicated previously, a dog is fed behind several screens standing in a series one after the other at a distance of not greater than half a meter, so that the dog has an image of food behind each of these screens. Therefore, if food is subsequently placed, within sight of the dog, behind one of these screens, or if the animal is led to one of them and shown the food there, then the maximum delay for running to it correctly is significantly decreased. This result is observed for visual and for auditory perception separately, as well as for complex perception. If the dog is released after a short interval of time of some minutes, it runs correctly to that screen at which it was last shown or allowed to eat food. But if it is released later, then the dog behaves differently; it goes to one of the screens, and if it does not find food there, it goes around to all of the remaining screens. This behavior occurs because the intensity of the psychoneural image to the most recently shown location of food wanes in the course of time and becomes comparable to some degree with the intensity of the psychoneural images of food in the remaining places. Therefore, following release from the cage, the dog runs indiscriminately to one of the feeders or wherever the image of food is projected.

It has been pointed out previously that the reproduction of the image of the perceived food object also occurs after cessation of circulation of excitation in the neural circuits, as well as after the period of increased excitability resulting from the presynaptic mediator. Reproduction of the image in the case of such a prolonged delay presumably originates, as was indicated previously, as a result of the effect of active protein in the postsynaptic regions; the active protein continuously maintains the postsynaptic membrane at some high level of ionic permeability. As has already been pointed out, this facilitates the distribution of excitation in the given neural circuits even if the afferent impulses appear from the effect of only a small part of the object or of its surroundings.

Thus, *image memory at different periods after each perception of the external object originates differently: Initially, in the first tens of seconds after the perception, the reproduction of the image occurs as a result of circulating excitation in neural circuits which had been activated during the perception; then, for some minutes it is determined in the main by an increased ionic permeability of membranes in the synaptic regions as the result of an increased secretion of mediator from the presynaptic terminations into the synaptic clefts, which occurs for some time after the cessation of reverberation of excitation; finally, the image is retained for a more or less long time, i.e., over many days or weeks, owing to the formation of stable active protein in the postsynaptic regions, which increases the ionic permeability of the postsynaptic membrane.*

Usually, short-term memory is termed operative, dynamic, or recent and is assumed to be on the basis only of reverberation of excitation in neuronal circuits. Long-term memory, on the other hand, is based on molecular changes of intracellular protein and is termed static or stable memory. It is in this sense that various authors, naturally enough, consider short-term and long-term memory as two absolutely different aspects of memory that are not at all related to one another. But actually, after each perception, there occur both reverberation of excitation in activated neural circuits and increased excitability from a presynaptic mediator, as well as a subsequent prolonged facilitatory condition from the postsynaptic protein-activator. Initially, all of these factors play a role in the reproduction of the image, in such a way that the presynaptic mediator and the active protein will be increased and the reverberation of excitation in neural circuits willl be prolonged. Therefore, during such reverberation, the image of the location of food must continually be located in front of the eyes. Upon cessation of the reverberation of excitation, the reproduction of the image of the place of food is dependent on facilitation of the transmission of excitation, under the influence of the presynaptic mediator and the postsynaptic protein-activator. But at this point, as has been indicated previously, the reproduction of the image will occur from time to time as a result of a new stimulating effect of one or another of the components of the surrounding environment. After the effect of the mediator ceases, the facilitatory effect of the protein-activator remains. In the latter case, the reproduction of the image must presumably originate upon perception of some component of the aspect of the location of the food.

On this basis, memory can be considered short-term when it is determined by reverberation of excitation, with a period of increased excitability resulting from the presynaptic mediator and facilitatory effect of the active protein. When memory is determined only by the action of the protein-activator, it can be considered long-term.

The question arises of whether the following fact is in agreement with this concept: Under certain conditions, short-term memory disappears temporarily, and long-term memory appears as it occurs after bilateral ablation of the inferior temporal lobes or the proreal gyri. As has been indicated previously, even though the dog after such an operation loses short-term memory, or the latter appears only for a few minutes, long-term memory can still be apparent; if the animal is given a piece of food in an absolutely new location, it will even go there the next day. Evidently, after one of the main links of the neural substrata of memory drops out, the reverberation of excitation upon each perception in the remaining neural substrata of memory is weakened and foreshortened significantly. This results in such a small increase in excitability in the given neural circuits as to be insufficient for short-term memory, i.e., so that this circuit is not activated by radiation of excitation evoked by the external stimulation. But such a weakening of reverberation of excitation is evidently sufficient for formation of stable active protein in such a quantity that it provides for long-term memory for some time—1 to 2 days, i.e., the image of food can be reproduced upon perception of the corresponding situation.

If the cybernetic term of code is used, then one can say that with long-term memory, the image of the perceived object is coded in the form of an intricate complex of association neural circuits that are activated upon perception of the particular object. In these neural circuits the secondary sensory areas, the proreal gyri, the inferior temporal lobes, and the hippocampus participate. In all of the excited association neurons of the particular circuit, active protein is synthesized. Therefore it occurs that, following removal of one of these substrata of memory, the ability to reproduce the image even for a delayed response does not disappear. The activation of association neurons of the remaining links turns out to be absolutely sufficient for evoking both the excitation of sensory stellate neurons that produce the image, and the projection pyramidal neurons that evoke the behavioral response.

Long-term memory, expressed as a behavioral response resulting from reproduction of the image of an object perceived only once a long time ago, is referred to in the literature as momentary training (Konorski, 1959), sensory training (Galambos and Morgan, 1956), or as "insight" (Köhler, 1929; Lashley, 1950). But none of these authors give this phenomenon of memory any kind of psychophysiological explanation. Gerard (1961), who dwells on the consideration of the origin of fixation of experiences, i.e., the retention of their traces for a long time, is again led to reverberation, i.e., to prolonged circulation of excitation in neural circuits and to the summation or progressive growth of structural changes, after each circulation of impulses of excitation along the neural circuit. These general considerations serve for an explanation of the elaboration of conditioned reflexes by means of practice, or the usual instrumental movements, but not for feeding behavior according to the image of a feeding object that had been perceived only once.

THE ROLE OF SUBCORTICAL STRUCTURES AND THE ORIGIN OF IMAGE MEMORY

In the origin of the phenomenon of memory in relation to the perception of objects of vital significance, an important role is played not only by cortical regions but also by subcortical structures such as the hypothalamus, the reticular formation, the caudate nucleus, and the cerebellum.

Reticular Formation. It is now well known that the level of cortical excitability is essentially dependent on the reticular formation. Thus, the rostral end of it, in the region of the upper half of the brain stem and the midbrain, has a desynchronizing effect on the spontaneous activity of the cerebral cortex, and a facilitatory effect on its primary responses (Moruzzi and Magoun, 1949; Magoun, 1958; Dumont and Dell, 1958; Bremer and Stoupel, 1959; Narikashvili et al., 1960, 1963, 1965). The same type of stimulation of certain regions of the lower bulbar reticular formation and the solitary nucleus, on the other hand, results in a synchronization of the spontaneous electrical activity of the cortex (Moruzzi and Magoun 1949; Narikashvili et al., 1965). Further, it is known that damage to the reticular formation results in a sharp reduction in the excitability of the cerebral cortex (Narikashvili, 1962); such damage also strongly impedes the formation and differentiation of conditioned reflexes (Lindsley *et al.*, 1950). Stimulation of the motor cortex, in turn, has a strong influence on the electrical activity of the brain stem, depressing slow waves to the level of extinction (Narikashvili, 1950, 1961). On the basis of well known facts, it can be concluded that the cortex and the reticular formation of the brain stem are connected both directly and *via* the diencephalon, i.e., thalamic and hypothalamic nuclei. It is through these connections that the inhibitory and facilitatory interactions between these structures must occur.

Further, it is well known that the nonspecific system arising from the reticular formation is basically connected with the secondary areas of the perceiving regions, and in general with the association fields. As was indicated previously, the secondary areas play an essential role in the establishment and retention of the image of the external world. Consequently, if, as acknowledged by Magoun (1958), Narikashvili (1962) and others, the association regions are the structures which are primarily and most easily activated by nonspecific impulses, then it can be concluded that nonspecific impulses are of major significance in the formation of the perception of images and other forms of psychic activity (see also Fuster, 1957, 1958; Fuster and Uyeda, 1962).

From the above discussion it clearly follows that damage to the reticular formation must strongly influence higher nervous activity. Experiments by Kediya, carried out on cats at our Institute of Physiology, have demonstrated that following bilateral lesions of the reticular formation in the mesencephalic region, conditioned reflexes are absent, and can be restored only after more than a month by means of a significantly larger number of reinforcements than prior to operation. Psychoneural activity is even more seriously disturbed. Short-term memory after a visual or a complex perception of the location of food reappears only after a month subsequent to operation, and then for not more than 30 sec; it then gradually improves but remains significantly poorer than prior to operation even after 7 months. In general, long-term memory is not restored. All of these effects must result from a decrease in the excitability of the cortex resulting from cessation or strong limitation of afferent impulses from the reticular formation.

Thus, it clearly follows that *normal activity of the reticular formation must be a necessary link in that complex neural activity on which the phenomenon of memory is dependent.*

The Lemniscal System, which constitutes the combined afferent system from skin and muscle receptors, must also play an important role in psychoneural memory. Bilateral injury of this system in the region of the midbrain results in a cessation of the flow of afferent impulses from the corresponding receptors and as a result, an impoverishment of cortical function necessarily ensues. Such animals are very similar to decorticate animals because of the pronounced diminution of neocortical function as reflected in perception, attention, and conditioned reflex activity. Emotional activity, especially, is strongly diminished (Sprague *et al.*, 1961).

According to our observations, after bilateral damage to the medial lemniscal system in cats, the emotional responses of fear and rage to noxious cutaneous stimuli are strongly diminished, and with more extensive lesions, are even absent. It is characteristic that such cats do not exhibit the responses of fear and rage even for visual stimuli such as the sight of a dog, for example (Tsintsadze, 1968). From these observations, it must be presumed that the emotional responses of fear and rage arise as a result of noxious or painful stimuli of the surface of the skin and constitute innate defensive responses. It is evident that on the basis of these responses, individually-acquired reactions of fear and rage arise when noxious agents are seen, e.g., in cats upon sight of a dog. This means that the sensory-integrative mechanisms of the emotional responses of rage and fear, which are located in the limbic system, are primarily (i.e., by means of an unconditioned pathway) excited through the diencephalon upon painful cutaneous stimulation, possibly even without participation of the reticular formation.

With bilateral lesions of the medial lemniscus in cats, short-term memory is disturbed for visual, auditory, labyrinthine, and also for complex perception of the location of food (Tsintsadze, 1968). The operated cats do not go to the place of food even 15 sec after perception of the latter.

Presumably, then, this disruption of short-term memory is dependent on a lowering of excitability of the cerebral cortex. Further, short-term memory actually returns to normal for about an hour after injection of caffeine (20%, 4 mg), i.e., it becomes the same as before operation.

Therefore, it can be emphasized that *defects of memory associated with damage to the lemniscal system basically result from a lowering of cortical activity generally, as a consequence of elimination of the continuous flow of afferent impulses from musculocutaneous receptors.*

The Caudate Nucleus. Detailed studies have recently been made of the role of the caudate nucleus and its head on delayed responses, i.e., on memory, but only in relation to conditioned reflex memory. It has been established that after bilateral removal of the head of the caudate nucleus, the same type of disturbance of memory is observed as occurs after ablation of the proreal gyri (Rosvold and Mishkin, 1961 and Rosvold and Szwarcbart, 1964). In addition, Nauta (1964) has pointed out their close anatomical connections. Evidently, the caudate nucleus participates in the phenomenon of memory as a result of its functional interaction with the cortex. It is well known that slow electrical stimulation (4 to 12 per sec) of the caudate nucleus in cats evokes slow potentials in the form of a recruiting response, and at the same time such stimulation leads to a somnolent state; the eyes are closed and do not respond to external stimuli. Stimulation of a higher frequency, on the other hand, produces a desynchronization of electrical activity and awakening. If the stimulation is still stronger, then the animal jumps to its feet, moves the head, and meows (Butkhuzi, 1963). With careful study of the electrical effects of the cortex in response to stimulation of the caudate nucleus, it was found that the desynchronizing, facilitatory effect affected predominantly the visual and auditory regions, and that this originated through the reticular formation of the midbrain. This means that impulses from the caudate nucleus reach the latter structure, and then *via* the ascending reticular system, arrive at the visual and auditory perceiving regions of the cerebral cortex. At the same time, such stimulation of the caudate nucleus has a synchronizing inhibitory effect predominantly on the sensorimotor region of the cortex. This effect originates in nonspecific thalamic nuclei (Butkhuzi, 1965).

It is further known that while stimulation of the caudate nucleus influences the perceiving regions of the cortex, stimulation of different perceiving regions of the cortex in turn activates the caudate nucleus. Upon stimulation of different regions of the cerebral cortex, potentials of a brief latent period are evoked in the caudate nucleus, which indicates the presence of direct connections from the cortex to the caudate nucleus (Butkhuzi, 1962). This connection between the cortex and the caudate nucleus is so close that an increase of activity in the cortical visual area as a result of strychninization is accompanied by an increase in the evoked potentials in the caudate nucleus and, on the other hand, a depression of cortical activity in the visual region as a result of hypothermia is accompanied by a decrease in the amplitude of evoked potentials in the caudate nucleus (Butkhuzi, 1965). Undoubtedly, the perceiving regions of the cortex and the caudate nucleus are interconnected by means of closed neural circuits that form a single integrated system. Therefore, the caudate nucleus must play an important role both in conditioned reflex activity and in psychoneural image activity of the cortex.

Experiments with bilateral destruction of the caudate nucleus in fact corroborate this suppostion. After such damage, an increased motor activity is observed as a result of the removal of the inhibitory influence from the caudate nucleus on the motor area. At the same time, a pronounced impairment for visual and auditory perception is apparent; delayed feeding behavior can occur only for 10 to 15 sec after perception of the location of food. From this fact we can conclude that the impairment of memory following damage to the caudate nucleus is determined by disappearance of its facilitatory effect on the visual and auditory areas of the cortex. We must suppose that for this reason the excitability of the secondary areas in these cortical regions is so diminished that the activity of association neural circuits cannot be sustained at a level such that the appearance of the image of the food location can occur. For the same reason, presumably, conditioned feeding behavior reflexes are disrupted for 4 or 5 weeks following very limited damage to the caudate nucleus (Ordzhonikidze, 1963), and disappear almost completely after extensive damage (Klosovskii and Volzhina, 1956).

It is now well known that visual and auditory stimuli activate not only the cortex but also the caudate nucleus (Albe-Fessard *et al.*, 1960). Consequently, with each visual and auditory perception, the visual and auditory regions of the cerebral cortex receive afferent impulses, in the first instance, directly from the specific system, and secondly, from the nonspecific system *via* the reticular formation, which is activated not only by direct impulses from the ascending sensory pathways, but also along complex pathways *via* the caudate nucleus. The latter link plays such an important role in cortical activity that following its removal, all individually acquired activity, in particular such higher forms of the latter as image psychoneural activity, is seriously impaired.

Thus, *the caudate nucleus and the perceiving regions of the cerebral cortex are mutually interrelated by means of two-way neural connections. Therefore, the caudate nucleus plays a significant role in the general facilitatory action by subcortical structures on the cortex, in particular, on the perceiving visual and auditory regions; it is thus instrumental in memory for auditory and visual perceptions.*

Cerebellum. As is well known, the cerebellum is a transmission station for a part of the ascending auditory and vestibular pathways. We know now that following removal of the posterior lobe of the cerebellum (the nodulo-flocculus and the uvula) and also the most anterior lobe (lingula), the functional activity of the cerebral cortex in relation to the projection of the objects perceived in external space, the establishment of spatial relations among these objects, and the production of orienting behavior toward them, is disturbed for a long time.

Immediately following the removal of these lobes of the cerebellum, or the entire cerebellum in the cat, the animal orients toward the striking of a food basin and can run to the place of the noise for food, both with closed eyes and with open eyes. But if the noise is stopped, the animal carries out searching movements but does not go to the source of the sound. In exactly the same way, the animal is not able, on the basis of labyrinthine receptors, to repeat the same path to the feeding place along which it had once been led with closed eyes. However, after 2 or 3 months this ability of image auditory and vestibular orientation is restored to a significant degree. Conditioned reflex activity to auditory and vestibular stimuli is also disturbed, but to a lesser degree and is restored sooner than image orientation to auditory and vestibular stimuli. Visual image activity is not significantly disturbed with damage to the cerebellum (Beritashvili, 1960).

On the basis of these facts it can be presumed that the cerebellum plays an important role in the implementation of the function of memory in relation to auditory and vestibular perception of the food object. It must be assumed that the cerebellum sends supplementary impulses to the auditory and vestibular perceiving areas of the cortex, *via* the reticular formation, with the effect that the excitability of sensory and association neurons is reinforced to a level necessary for recall of auditory and vestibular perceptions.

This premise is supported by the fact that stimulation of the cerebellum in the region of the nodulus, the flocculus, and the uvula produces primary responses in those same regions of the cortex as does stimulation of the labyrinthine and auditory receptors, i.e., in the temporal lobe, primarily in the anterior part of the ectosylvian and suprasylvian gyri (Kempinsky, 1951; Mickle and Ades, 1954). Stimulation of the paramedial and the anterior lobes, on the other hand, evokes primary responses in the sensorimotor cortex (Bekaya and Moniava, 1963).

It is also known that activity of the cerebral cortex has a specific effect on the electrical activity of the cerebellum, resulting in the appearance in the latter of slow potentials similar to the alpha rhythm (8 to 10 per sec) as in the cerebral cortex (Tskipuridze and Bakuradze, 1948).

The cerebellum is also directly connected with the reticular formation, and *via* that formation it is connected with the paleocortex. It is known that stimulation of the cerebellum evokes electrical potentials of varying duration in the paleocortex (Bekaya and Moniava, 1963). Stimulation of the cerebellum produces a depression of the electrical activity of the brain stem; stimulation of the latter, on the other hand, has a facilitatory effect on electrical responses of the cerebellum (Narikashvili *et al.*, 1963). There evidently exist bilateral neuronal connections between these parts of the brain (Narikashvili, 1950; Brodal, 1957; and others). It is fundamental to emphasize that the effect of the cerebellum on the cerebral cortex is implemented, in relation to the neocortex, *via* nuclei of the midbrain and the ventromedial thalamic nuclei, but in relation to the paleocortex *via* the reticular formation (Bekaya and Moniava, 1963).

Stimulation of different parts of the cerebellum also influences the caudate nucleus, evoking electrical potentials in it bilaterally. This effect is indirect, for it disappears upon administering nembutal (Butkhuzi, 1962).

Thus, *the cerebellum is a part of a very complex system of neural circuits that includes the reticular formation, the caudate nucleus, the nuclei of the midbrain and the diencephalon. By means of activation of this system, the cerebellum exerts a facilitatory effect on the cerebral cortex, especially the auditory and vestibular regions, which is strongly conducive to memory of auditory and vestibular perceptions.*

The question now arises of what role each link of these circuits plays in the phenomena of memory. With respect to the proreal gyrus (the secondary area of the gustatory region) it is known that, as the substratum of memory, it is in close two-way connection with subcortical structures, in particular, the caudate nucleus and the cerebellum. Therefore, activity of the substratum of memory must also depend to some extent on afferent impulses arriving from the cerebellum, primarily *via* the reticular formation and the ascending reticular system, and secondly, *via* "association" thalamic nuclei and thalamocortical connections.

CHARACTERISTICS AND ORIGIN OF EMOTIONAL MEMORY

In its basic form, memory must also be concerned with the remembering of specific emotional circumstances upon repetition of the influence of that situation in which the given emotional circumstances had originally been experienced. This phenomenon of memory was studied in relation to the emotions of fear and hunger.

Memory of the Emotion of Fear. If a cat or dog is subjected to painful stimulation while eating, i.e., when the food touches the mouth, then the cat runs away from the feeder, yowling and bristling, and the dog, yelping. Subsequently, these animals will not spontaneously approach the particular feeder, not only the same day, but even after many weeks. If, for example, automatic feeding behavior in response to sound or light had been elaborated toward this feeder in a dog, then for many weeks after this single electrical stimulation, the animal will respond to this conditional signal by pricking up the ears, remaining fixed in the same place, but will not approach the feeder (Bregadze, 1948 Beritashvili, 1961).

If automatic feeding behavior has been elaborated in a cat or dog to two different feeders in response to different signals, then after electrical stimulation while eating from one of the feeders, for many days the fear response is evoked, but only in response to the corresponding conditional signal. The other conditional feeding signal, corresponding to the other feeder, does not evoke the response of fear, and the animal runs to that feeder when it is signaled (Bregadze, 1948).

As has been shown by Oniani and Orjonikidze (1968) and Naneishvili (1967), a burst of activity of a rhythm of 35 to 40 waves per second arise in the basolateral part of the amygdaloid complex and in the pyriform gyrus during the emotional responses of pricking up the ears, restlessness, and fear.

The amplitude of these waves varies in proportion to the intensity of the external stimulus for the emotional response. This burst of electrical activity is observed both with direct stimulation of the paleocortex so as to evoke the response of fear, as well as in response to conditional signals that evoked that emotional response. It is noteworthy that such electrical activity (35 to 40 per sec) was observed by these authors in hungry animals upon being shown food or during conditional feeding signals which evoked a response of running to the feeder.

It is evident that this burst of electrical activity reflects not the activity of sensory-emotional neurons, but of association neurons, which connect these sensory neurons with efferent motor neurons that produce the external manifestation of the emotion.

As is known, during electrical stimulation of the cingulate and hippocampal gyri, and also the amygdala and the pyriform lobe, by means of in-dwelling electrodes, the same response of fear ensues as for strong painful stimulation of the skin (MacLean, 1957; Nutsubidze, 1961; Naneishvili, 1967). After bilateral destruction of one of these parts of the cortex, the response of fear to stimulation of the skin, and in general to any other kind of influence, is temporarily appreciably diminished (MacLean, 1957; Nutsubidze, 1961, 1963). We suppose that the sensory neurons of the emotional response of fear, which are probably the stellate cells with short axons, are located in the paleocortex and are integrated by the internuncial and association pyramidal neurons of the paleocortex. This sensory structure must be found in bilateral connections with the integrative mechanism of emotional behavior. This integration is accomplished by association and intermediary pyramidal neurons of the archipaleocortex. It is evident that the same kind of active protein is synthesized in these association neurons as in the neocortex, and thus determines the appearance of stable connections of the sensory elements sustaining fear with the integrative mechanisms of the external response to the latter.

It must be presumed that in the normal animal the entire sensory neuronal association structure leading to fear readily interconnects, from the very first time, with both the perceiving neurons of the paleocortex and those in the neocortex which are excited by different types of stimuli from the external world at the time of the painful stimulation. Therefore, the response of fear is evoked not only by the influence of the external world on the paleocortex directly, but also *via* the neocortex, or even primarily *via* the neocortex.

The normal cat or dog, after electrical stimulation during eating, is afraid of the entire environment during stimulation, in particular, of that feeder at which the stimulation had taken place. This response, which is an unconditioned one, occurs by means of the archipaleocortex, but necessarily entails the reproduction of the projection externally of the image of the feeder at which stimulation had occurred. It must be presumed that following the formation of connections between the neo- and paleocortex upon the very first trial of the experience with the noxious agent, the neocortex responds with the emotion of fear by means of transmission of impulses of excitation from the neocortical psychoneural complex for the given image to the sensori-integrative mechanism of fear in the limbic system.

It is characteristic that analogous conversion of a positive feeding signal into a negative one that evokes the response of fear is observed in cats deprived of the neocortex following its extirpation. In such cats, both short-term and long-term image memory is completely lacking. In relation to the emotional response of fear, however, memory is not lacking but is only severely impaired. If strong electrical stimulation is applied at the time of eating evoked by the conditional signal, the cat jumps away from the feeder and remains rigid for several minutes. It would not approach the feeder in response to a conditional signal even if the latter was applied after the end of the arrest reaction; if it is brought to the feeder, it turns aside and does not eat the food. Fear elicited by the conditional signal persists for several days in some operated animals. It can be stated that if the neocortex is separated from the remaining part of the brain by sectioning of all afferent and efferent pathways using the method of Khananashvili (1961), then long-term emotional memory almost completely disappears. It is only for a few minutes that the animal does not take food from the feeder, and starts to eat again 5 to 10 min later. It must be presumed that the animal does not approach the feeder, even in response to the conditional signal as long as fear persists. If after extirpation of the neocortex, the usual result is not observed, an incomplete removal is implied.

It is evident that in cats deprived of the neocortex, upon painful stimulation, a reverberation of excitation between sensory elements of fear, the apparatus which integrates the outward manifestations of fear, and those neurons which are excited by the environmental stimulation begins in the paleocortex. This excitation is not experienced subjectively. Evidently, sensory neurons of the archipaleocortex that perceive different types of auditory, visual, or cutaneous stimuli respond similarly to the neocortex to proprioceptive and visceral stimulation, without a definite differentiation of the subjective sensation. Although cats without the neocortex distinguish light from darkness, they nonetheless run into obstacles. This means that upon reverberation of excitation, they are excited together with sensory neurons of fear and those neurons which integrate the external response of fear, without the emergence of the image of the entire situation of the painful stimulation. This reverberation of excitation persists for some time after the painful stimulation, during which time the subjective experience is produced as well as the outward manifestations of fear. When the reverberation of excitation ceases, the response of fear disappears. But in all of the synaptic apparatus of the neurons activated by it, the increased excitability persists for some time, owing to the formation of presynaptic vesicles containing mediators. This condition lasts for minutes, and during this time sensory neurons for fear and for integrating the outward response of fear can easily be activated anew by one or the other of the external aspects of the stimulation. This condition of increased excitability does, however, subside after a few minutes; after 10 to 20 min, the response of fear in front of the feeder disappears and is no longer apparent either on the same day, or on the following days. From this it follows that *cats deprived of the neocortex are capable of short-term emotional memory, but not of long-term emotional memory.* However, this short-term recall is accomplished without reproduction of the image of the location of the noxious agent.

Thus, *in normal animals, memory for emotional stimulation of fear is based on a momentary coupling of neocortical sensory elements perceiving the external world with the sensori-intergrative mechanism of fear located in the archipaleocortex. The activity of this connection, with its subjective and objective manifestations, is presumably controlled by the psychoneural complex of the image of location of the noxious agent.*

Animals deprived of the neocortex also possess memory for the emotion of fear, but here the memory is brought about in the archipaleocortex by means of coupling of its neural elements that perceive the elements of painful stimulation with the sensori-integrative mechanism of fear which is excited by such a stimulus. Such connections must also be formed in the normal animal, but their activity will be regulated by the neocortex according to the image of the location of the noxious agent.

In normal animals, the basis of retention of the emotional response of fear from a single experience of the noxious agent perhaps also lies in the formation of active protein in the postsynaptic portions of association pyramidal cells of the archipaleocortex, on which terminate the association pathways from the neocortex excited by the noxious agent. As in the neocortex, this protein probably plays an essential role in the transmission of excitation in the postsynaptic portions.

As is known, upon stimulation of certain parts of the hippocampus, both feeding behavior and defensive flight occur. Moreover, with each behavioral act a generalized inhibition occurs, which depresses both conditioned reflexes and to some degree unconditioned ones, i.e., entirely purposeful behavior is evoked from the hippocampus.

Removal or, more correctly, damage to the hippocampus strongly influences emotional behavior, diminishing or enhancing one or another form of behavior, depending on the site of the injury. For example, with bilateral injury of the posterior part of the hippocampus, the response of fear disappears, even for electrical stimulation of the skin of the animal. If during eating, the nostrils are stimulated electrically, the cat does not cease eating, nor run away from the feeder, nor does it cease approaching the feeder subsequently.

When the hippocampus is subjected to strong electrical stimulation or when an active neuronal poison, such as carbocholine, is applied locally, it produces prolonged convulsive electrical discharges which quickly spread to the entire limbic system, both ipsilaterally and contralaterally. During this time, the animal ceases responding to painful stimulation of the skin of the paw, and also loses memory for conditioned defensive movement of the paw in response to conditional auditory signals. During these convulsions, the heart and respiration also cease to respond to such conditional and unconditional stimulation (Flynn, MacLean, and Kim, 1961). It is evident that the absence of unconditioned and conditioned defensive reflexes, and also vegetative changes to conditional and unconditional stimuli, are dependent on strong excitation of efferent neurons of the hippocampus, at the time of these convulsive discharges, which produce inhibition of the subcortical mechanisms of somatovegetative responses. As is known, inhibition ensues under all conditions of stimulation in the dorsal part of the hippocampus. It is evident that while a generalized convulsive discharge is elicited, generalized inhibition occurs because of involvement of the dorsal part of the hippocampus.

It is characteristic that in the experiments of MacLean and his coworkers, convulsive discharges arising in the hippocampus do not spread to the neocortex. They presumably also do not affect the transmitting nuclei of the specific system, since auditory stimulation evokes primary electrical responses in the auditory cortex during such convulsions, as in the normal. From this result it must be presumed that the defect of memory in relation to emotional stimulation of fear which is observed during convulsive excitation of the hippocampus bilaterally is dependent on an inhibitory condition of the archipaleocortex.

It is well known that the emotion of fear is also dependent on the anterior parts of the cingulate gyri. When the latter are stimulated, the cat draws up, turns to the opposite side, and the feeding response is inhibited; the cat ceases eating and does not resume feeding as long as stimulation is continued (Koridze, 1967). The response of fear can be generated to sound and light if these stimuli are combined with electrical stimulation of the cingulate gyrus (Nutsubidze, 1961; Koridze, 1967). From this it can be concluded that *the sensory elements of fear are located mainly in the cingulate gyrus and the pyriform lobe. Memory in relation to the response of fear and its integration must in essence be dependent on the hippocampal gyrus.*

The response of fear, with all its outward manifestations, also appears upon stimulation of subcortical structures: the amygdala, hypothalamus, thalamus, midbrain and bulbar reticular formation. Conditioned responses of fear to indifferent stimuli are formed on the basis of these structures. The environment in which the painful stimulation is produced also evokes a response of fear (Delgado *et al.*, 1956; Mandell and Bach, 1952; Nakao, 1959; Romaniuk, 1964; and others). These responses of fear to the external circumstances are undoubtedly evoked from the paleocortex, where the sensory neurons of fear are located. However, upon repetition of the effect of the painful stimulus, these neurons are activated *via* the neocortex, which, as was discussed previously, establishes long-term connections with association neurons of the integrative apparatus for fear in the paleocortex.

It is characteristic that when the hippocampus is stimulated, together with small movements of the head, there is also an inhibition of conditioned motor reflexes elaborated on the basis of movement of the extremity resulting from stimulation of the motor zone of the cerebral cortex. To a lesser degree, unconditioned reflexes evoked by electrical stimulation of the cortex are also inhibited. According to experiments of my co-worker Tevzadze, stimulation of the hippocampus is followed by an inhibitory aftereffect measured in hours.

Ordinarily, threshold stimulation of the hippocampus evokes those movements of the head which are characteristic of an attitude of concentrated attention and recollection, i.e., the animal remains fixated in a particular stance (Lissak and Grastyan., 1957). This external manifestation also supports the supposition that the hippocampus must be the basic substratum of memory in relation to the emotion of fear, i.e., the active protein formed in association neurons of the hippocampus under the influence of impulses of excitation from the neocortex enables both revival of the emotion of fear and also the excitation of the particular efferent pyramidal neurons which result in a prolonged inhibitory effect on the motor apparatus.

The Impossibility of Reproduction of Pain. When the animal experiences the effect of a noxious agent, it not only experiences the emotion of fear and the tendency to run away from that environment, but it must also feel pain. We well know this from our own subjective experience of noxious stimulation. But it is characteristic that when the same environment is subsequently encountered but without painful stimulation, man experiences an unpleasant sensation of fear, but does not feel pain. Evidently, indifferent stimuli of the environment are not coupled with those neuronal elements which produce the sensation of pain. According to the prevailing opinion, special sensory elements exist in the paleocortex which are activated by ascending paths conducting volleys from pain receptors. It is presumed that pain receptors in the form of nerve terminations are located in all organs of the body and that more or less strong stimulation of them, whether mechanical, chemical, or electrical, evokes the sensation of pain. Moreover, when we established a conditioned defensive reflex in man to an indifferent stimulus by means of reinforcement by strong painful electrical stimulation of the leg, then after some number of combinations, the indifferent stimulus evoked shivering of the entire body, an unpleasant creepy sensation of "goose pimples" along the spine, but not one of the subjects experienced pain either from stimulation of the leg nor from any other part of the body (Beritashvili and Dzidzishvili, 1934).

The question thus arises of why is pain never reproduced as a response to pairing an indifferent stimulus with it. If indeed there exist sensory neurons which, when excited by painful stimulation, result in the subjective sensation of pain, then these neurons must have become associated with the indifferent stimuli and are excited by the paired indifferent stimulus, as always occurs with the emotion of fright. It seems to me that the following kind of explanation suggests itself. Sensory neurons subserving pain in the paleocortex are adapted to those afferent impulses which arise from pain receptors. The latter impulses are very distinctive: they are of low amplitude, long duration (approaching 10 msec), and low frequency (Dzidzishvili, 1948). Correspondingly, the lability of these sensory cells must be very low. Therefore tactile, muscular, auditory, and other impulses do not evoke pain, since they are of short duration ($\frac{1}{2}$ to 1 msec) and do not excite these sensory cells. It is probable that, for the same reason, they cannot become conditional signals for pain. But of course with a pathological increase of excitability in sensory cells for pain such as occurs in causalgia, i.e., when the excitability of these cells is strongly increased from prolonged stimulation of a damaged sensory nerve, any stimulus can evoke pain. However, this phenomenon is not related to memory.

Memory of the Emotion of Hunger. In man, the sensations of hunger and satiation are accompanied by the subjective experience of hunger and satiation, respectively. The same must occur in higher vertebrates, but we should base our assumption on absolutely clear outward manifestations of these sensations. Under conditions of hunger, animals go about restlessly, sniffing all objects until they find food. After satiation, these searching movements cease, the animal becomes settled, lies down and begins to drowse.

It is now well known that there exist parts of the paleocortex, the electrical stimulation of which (in chronic experiments with indwelling electrodes) evokes feeding behavior in the hungry animal. Thus, with stimulation of different parts of the pyriform gyrus, profuse salivation and masticatory movements ensue, the animal gets up, sniffs the floor, and, finding food, begins to eat it. The same also results under conditions of satiation (Oniani and Ordzhonikidze., 1968). On the other hand, upon stimulation of other parts, e.g., the entorhinal part of the pyriform gyrus or the anterior half of the basolateral part of the amygdaloid complex, the animal ceases to eat.

The question arises of whether it is possible to evoke the emotion of hunger and satiation, with their outward manifestation, from memory by some kind of external indifferent stimulation. It is now well known that these emotional responses normally arise from specific chemical shifts in the *milieu interne*. The basic coordinating apparatus for implementing feeding behavior and for the state of satiety is found in the medial and lateral hypothalamus, respectively. It is found that if a sympathetic substance such as acetylcholine or a similar carbocholine product is artificially introduced into the lateral hypothalamus, an animal that had been satisfied beforehand to the point of refusal of food begins to eat anew (Miller, 1965).

Analogous neural mechanisms, presumably, also exist for the sensation of thirst and for satisfaction of it. For the present, the role of the archipaleocortex in relation to thirst is not known. However, we do know that the hypothalamus plays as important a role in relation to thirst as it does in relation to hunger. Thus, if a solution of sodium chloride of a somewhat higher concentration than is present in the body fluids is injected in the lower medial part of the hypothalamus of the dog, the animal begins to drink, carrying out the usual motions of obtaining water. This occurs even if the animal had previously drunk to the point of refusal. If at that time pure water is injected, the opposite effect ensues; the animal ceases drinking (Miller, 1965).

All of these substances that evoke hunger and thirst presumably also act similarly on other nuclei of the limbic system which participate in the complex neuronal circuits upon which the satisfaction of thirst and hunger depends. It is thus evident that there exist corresponding complex systems of neural circuits in the limbic system for the satisfaction of both the needs of eating and of drinking, such that each system possesses specific characteristics of response to specific chemical effects. All of these chemical shifts are based on an insufficiency of food and water in the gastrointestinal tract. Following intake of food and water of sufficient quantity, these shifts in the blood disappear and another type of chemical shift ensues, in response to the presence of a sufficient quantity of food and water in the gastrointestinal tract. It must be presumed that in the absence of the corresponding chemical excitation no somatic stimulus (visual, auditory, musculocutaneous, or olfactory) can excite the sensory neurons of sensation of hunger and thirst, nor the neurons of the circuits for satisfaction of hunger and thirst. Therefore, they cannot serve for calling forth the sensation of hunger and thirst by means of neural pathways from memory, but they can easily result from a temporary connection with motor mechanisms of satisfaction of needs of food and drink. Since activation of these mechanisms results in conditions of hunger and thirst of the animal, then it is clear that each external stimulus can become a conditional feeding signal when it is combined with the act of eating, as has also been shown experimentally. But if a satiated animal is repeatedly led to a new place of food, to the accompaniment of some indifferent sound, and does not eat, no conditioned reflex of running to this place of food is formed either to this sound or to the entire situation of the experiment (Aivazashvili, 1963).

Moreover, if a conditioned feeding reflex has been formed on the basis of feeding of a hungry animal, then it ceases to be evoked when the animal is satiated. This means that in the absence of the corresponding chemical shift in the *milieu interne*, the neural circuits for satisfying hunger and thirst are not excited by an external stimulus evidently as a result of a pronounced decrease of excitability. But if the circuits are excited under the influence of electrical stimulation, then the excitation evidently occurs with considerable intensity. Consequently, one cannot speak of memory for the sensation of hunger and thirst in the same manner as for an individually-acquired emotion, which can be produced under the influence of the situation in which the gratification of the sensation of hunger and thirst occurred.

Thus, *the subjective sensations of hunger and thirst, which arise only in conditions of hunger and thirst by means of innate pathways and in relation to chemical shifts in the blood, disappear following satiation and satisfaction of thirst as a result of the corresponding changes in the chemical constitution of the blood. They cannot be evoked by a conditioned reflex pathway or by the influence of the image of the object associated with feeding and drinking.*

Memory of the Emotion of Sex. The emotion of sex is also dependent on activation of specific sensory neurons of the limbic system under the influence of sexual hormones. It is now known that the artificial introduction of sexual hormones (testosterone in the male and estrogen in the female) into specific parts of the limbic system of the rat, e.g., in the preoptic region, calls forth the entire behavioral response of male and female sexual behavior —satisfaction of sexual need and reproduction. These hormones do not evoke active behavior in other parts of the brain (Miller, 1960, 1965). Presumably, sexual hormones increase the sensitivity and thereupon also excite specific sensory elements in the limbic system which produce the subjective experience of the emotion of sex. Only under such conditions do these sensory elements become able to respond to specific external stimulation with a heightened sexual excitability and by satisfaction of sexual desire. The behavioral manifestations of these emotions must depend in both sexes on peripheral excitation of the sex organs and on the specific type of stimulation from the environment which must serve for satisfaction of maternity and the nurturing of offspring. These peripheral influences act initially as unconditional stimuli by means of an innate pathway. But in higher vertebrates, after repetition of both these and other associated stimuli, the image of the sexual object with whom coitus had occurred, or the image of offspring and their external attributes, or their dwelling place can be evoked. Therefore, it can be said that sexual behavior of higher vertebrates is basically regulated by means of such image psychoneural activity. Later, after multiple repetitions all of these stimuli become conditional signals to the specific act of sexual behavior or of caring for offspring. Since these images are retained for a long time, then, correspondingly, they can be reproduced under the influence of one or another component of that situation in which coitus or the nurturing of offspring had occurred.

Thus, *memory of the emotion of sex in both its subjective aspect and in its behavioral manifestations can be evident in the presence of the corresponding sexual hormone in the limbic system, i.e., in its neural formations having sexual functions.*

CHARACTERISTICS AND ORIGIN OF LONG-TERM CONDITIONED REFLEX MEMORY

Characteristics of Learned Activity. A basic form of memory is apparent in the prolonged retention of learned motion in the form of habits and conditioned reflexes. Habitual or so-called learned instrumental movements are initially regulated by the image of the very movements of the particular extremity. If a cat or dog while searching for food opens the feeder by accidental pressure of the paw on some device (lever), then an image not only of the location of the feeder, but also of those motions of the paw which opened the feeder, is formed in the animal. Therefore, these instrumental movements in the form of pressure of the paw on the lever are initially regulated by the psychoneural process of the image of these movements. Evidently, the neural circuits of the psychoneural process of this image are established by means of musculocutaneous and labyrinthine perception of those movements during pressure on the lever. In this process, the head and the eyes were naturally fixed on the lever and on the paw that was moving. Therefore, the aforesaid neural circuit must include pyramidal projection neurons for both the production of the given movement of the paw and also for the corresponding orienting movements of the head and eyes. It is clear that the opening of the feeder is initially regulated by the aforementioned psychoneural processes, but subsequently, after the feeder has been opened many times, temporary connections between the sight of the lever and the pressing of it by the paw must have been elaborated, as a consequence of which a conditioned reflex arises in the form of pressing the lever upon seeing it.

We hold that exactly the same psychoneural phase obtains for elaboration of a conditional salivary or defensive reflex. Upon the first reinforcements of an indifferent stimulus with food, the latter evokes an orienting response in the form of extending the head and movement in the direction of the feeder, under the influence of the reproduction of the image of the location of food. Only after many reinforcements with food does the indifferent stimulus become a conditional signal for the given movement, by means of formation of the corresponding temporary connections (Beritashvili, 1947) and, undoubtedly, the salivary secretion which is observed after a few combinations must be of a psychoneural nature, evoked by the image of the location of the food. We know that when the hungry dog visits a familiar place of food, at which it has eaten only once, the animal secretes saliva (Beritashvili and Kalabegashvili, 1944).

The same can be said with respect to the formation of conditioned defensive reflexes by means of combination of an indifferent stimulus with painful stimulation of the skin of the extremities. Upon painful stimulation, the head turns to the side of the stimulus and the eyes fixate on the part of the skin stimulated; the animal whines, draws back quickly, respiration quickens, and after several strong stimuli, the animal attempts to free itself from the platform on which it had been standing.

When the indifferent stimulus is repeated without reinforcement with a painful stimulus, the animal initially responds as for the painful stimulus, or even more strongly. This response is undoubtedly of psychoneural origin and ensues after the very first pairing, *via* the paleocortex in the form of the emotion of fear, as has already been noted. Moreover, there must occur a reproduction of the image of the place of stimulation of the skin and of lifting the paw in the animal.

But after multiple pairings, the emotion of fear with its behavioral manifestations in response to the conditional stimuli gradually wanes and subsequently disappears almost entirely. The latter is usually the case if the painful stimulus was applied during the conditional signal but only in the absence of defensive movements. In response to the conditional signal, the animal raised only one foot and turned the head slightly to the side of this extremity (Beritashvili, 1932). But since with each reinforcement of the conditional stimulus by the unconditional stimulus, the entire surroundings also act on the receptors of the individual, and since muscle and joint receptors also begin to be excited in the corresponding response that ensues, then temporary connections can be formed between the focus of the unconditional stimulus not only in response to the conditional stimulus, but to the entire situation or to individual components of it. From this it is clear that various perceiving regions participate in the formation of temporary connections, and there is an amalgamation of their fields. Thus, for example, in the formation of a conditioned avoidance flexion of the leg as a result of pairing of some indifferent tone with stimulation of the extremity, the auditory, cutaneous, motor, and vestibular regions of the cortex must participate in the formation of temporary connections, for in response to electrical stimulation of the extremity, motion of the legs and the head ensue; the dog raises the leg and turns the head in the direction of the stimulus. All of these primary and secondary stimuli also act upon the association fields of the neocortex *via* activation of the reticular formation. Moreover, electrical stimulation evokes pain and certain external responses of fear from the paleocortex. Consequently, certain neural nuclei of the archipaleocortex are excited with each pairing of the stimuli. Also, in the elaboration of a conditioned defensive reflex, all of the parts mentioned, of course, participate. Temporary connections are formed between all of these excited parts of the new and the old cortex. Usually, however, we study the formation of a defensive reflex by observation of movement of the extremity, or by the electrical activity of the neocortex in the perceiving areas for the conditioned and the unconditioned stimuli.

These simple and complex learned responses appear not only on the day of elaboration, but also on the following day or still later. They can be evoked, although in a weakened form, many weeks and months after their last reinforcement with an unconditional reflex. These individually elaborated responses are essentially expressions of a particular type of long-term memory which is based not on the perceived image of the location of food, but on the activation of temporary connections elaborated by practice. The duration of retention of learned or conditional reflex movement depends basically on the extent of practice, i.e., on how long and how frequent these learned movements are repeated; the more frequent the repetition, the longer they are retained.

Origin of Learned Activity. As is known, after repeated combinations of a conditional stimulus within an unconditional one, two-way temporary connections are developed between neuronal complexes which perceive these stimuli (Beritashvili, 1927, 1932). However, the development of temporary connections upon the formation of conditioned reflexes and learned movements, in general, must depend on development of synaptic structures in the association neurons constituting the temporary connections.

The external response which occurs as a result of the temporary connections must originate *via* projectional pyramidal and extrapyramidal neurons, from which it can be presumed that the external manifestations of conditioned or learned responses are also based, perhaps mainly, on the structural development of the synaptic apparatus of these projectional neurons.

The structural development of the synaptic apparatus may also be apparent in the formation of new synaptic endings by means of branching of strongly activated presynaptic fibers in the brain of adult animals, as has been shown by Edds (1965), Kruger (1965), and Kuparadze (1965) and even earlier by Ramon y Cajal (1959) in the process of postembryonic development of the CNS. Finally, the development of the synaptic apparatus can also be evident in the activation of those synapses which in general do not affect the formation of a conditioned reflex. The presence of such potential synapses is affirmed by many authors (Haggar and Barr, 1950; Eccles, 1964; Barondes, 1965). It is possible that chemical shifts in the intercellular space, resulting from reinforced activation of neural and glial cells may play a certain role in these structural changes. In passing, it should be noted that such chemical shifts do act on nerve fibers, promoting growth and budding of the latter. Presumably, the same chemical conditions are established as in injured regions of the spinal column or in the cerebral cortex. As is known, posterior root fibers in the spinal column give off a set of collaterals to the degenerating neuron when there is any kind of damage to the transynaptic neurons (Ramon y Cajal, 1959; Purpura, 1961; for details see Sharpless, 1964).

It is now well known that axoplasm possesses the ability of ameboid movement (Kuparadze, 1965, and others). Therefore, potential synapses can become active or they can appear on presynaptic fibers as buds which then elongate, forming filaments with a vesicle at the end. If a cell is nearby, these vesicles presumably form synapses upon coming into contact with the cell.

According to data of Kuparadze (1965), the sensorimotor area for the forelimb of the dog is characterized by a clearcut structural change around the pyramidal cells in layer V after formation of a simple defensive motor reflex in this leg. In the intercellular space, numerous newly formed synaptic collaterals appear: myelinated fibers with bud-like formations and collaterals with bead-like thickenings. Moreover, a slight swelling of the pyramidal neurons is observed, two or three nucleolar inclusions appear in the pyramidal cells, and apical and basal dendrites become somewhat entwined (Fig. 10).

But what is especially characteristic, in the internuncial pyramidal neurons, which transmit exitation from association fibers of the area perceiving the conditional signal to the association neurons of the motor zone (B_{18} and B_{19} in Fig. 10), the quantities of amino acids, lipoproteins, and SH-groups of proteins decrease in various degrees, and their axons become

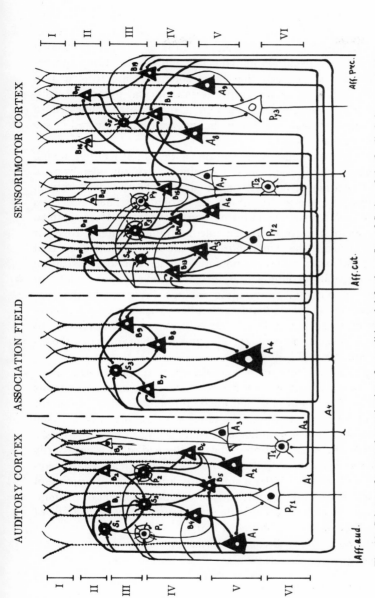

Fig. 10. Schema of neuronal organization of a conditioned-defensive reflex of flexing of the forelimb in response to sound. The unconditioned-defensive reflex is evoked by electrical stimulation of the limb. Temporary connections are shown between neurons of the auditory, cutaneous, and motor regions, and also the association fields; the axons of the neurons which participate in temporary connections are indicated by heavy lines. A_1 to A_9—association pyramidal neurons, the axons of which connect different parts of the cortex via the white matter; B_1 to B_{19}—internuncial pyramidal neurons, the axons of which do not leave the cortex; S_1 to S_5—transmission stellate cells; P_1 to P_4—stellate sensory cells, among which P_1 and P_4 do not have axonal connections with pyramidal neurons; P_{y1} to P_{y3}—projection pyramidal neurons, the axons of which project to other parts of the brain; T_1 and T_2—neurons of Martinotti, the axons of which rise vertically to layer I; Aff_{cut}—afferents from the surface of the skin; Aff_{prc}—afferents from muscles, tendons, and joints. All of the regions shown are connected by association neurons by the subcortical white matter, but only cutaneous and motor regions are additionally connected by transcortical internuncial pyramidal neurons B_{15} and B_{18}.

enriched with amino acids. Moreover, a doubling or tripling of satellite glia and a doubling of capillaries is observed around all of these cells (Kuparadze and Kostenko, 1968). It can be assumed that the presynaptic fibers with newly formed collaterals terminate on association cells (among which are included the aforementioned internuncial pyramidal cells), and also on newly appearing glial cells. It may be assumed that these collaterals are formed as a result of metabolic processes occurring in the internuncial pyramidal cells. Kuparadze observed all of these changes in a motor area subjected to corresponding training procedures. These changes were not observed in the contralateral motor area (Fig. 11).

Considering a neuronal-glial organization of the CNS, Roitbak (1968, 1969) proposed a hypothesis concerning a specific role of oligodendrocytes in the structural development of the synaptic apparatus. As is well known, oligodendrocytes possess the ability of myelin formation. Their processes wrap around axons and form a myelin membrane on the latter. It is presumed that with activation of the cortex by an unconditional stimulus, together with excitation of neurons the oligodendrocytes are also activated, so that their membrane depolarizes and slow potentials arise. This depolarization is a signal of their myelin-forming activity around newly formed collaterals and around fibers of potential presynaptic endings. As a result, the conduction of impulses along all of these nerve fibers is enhanced and correspondingly there must be a significant intensification of the release of mediators from the presynaptic vesicles. This process then increases the effectiveness of transmission of excitation.

It has been established that in the elaboration of a conditioned reflex, those functional and structural developments which occur in neural circuits with each pairing of the conditional and unconditional stimuli continue for some minutes following each pairing. Therefore, if in the intervals between the pairings, some type of strong influence occurs such as anoxia, narcosis, or electroshock, then the consolidation of the conditioned reflex is necessarily impeded, since the activity of temporary connections and their synaptic apparatus is thereby switched off. After a sufficiently long period of training of the conditioned reflex, i.e., after a sufficiently strong development of the temporary connections, the same external influences do not affect the activity of these connections (Burešova and Bureš, 1963).

Thus, *at the present time, it can be considered most probable that the basic structural changes of the synaptic apparatus during formation of temporary connections include the multiplication of presynaptic endings and satellite glia, as well as intensified myelinization of presynaptic fibers.*

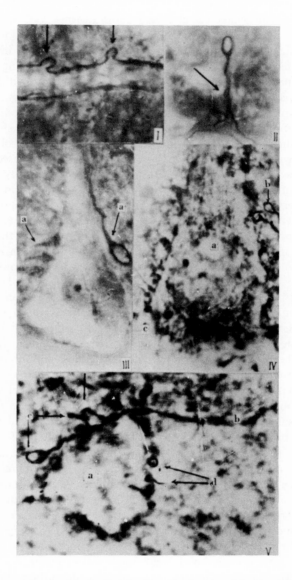

Fig. 11. Motor area for the right forelimb in the cerebral cortex of the dog following formation of a conditioned-defensive reflex of the left forelimb. Middle complex of the layers. I—Bud-like invaginations into the substance of a fiber. II—newly formed collateral of a myelinated fiber. III—pyramidal cell with newly formed synaptic endings. IV—(a) pyramidal cell, (b) termination of newly formed collaterals, (c) presynaptic thickening. V—(a) neuron; (b) newly formed collateral, (c) thickening along a collateral and on a free ending, (d) synaptic bouton and annulus on the surrounding cell. Unstained material. Magnification × 1800 (Kuparadze, 1965).

Molecular and Submolecular Changes with Learned Activity. In the origin of long-term memory in relation to conditioned reflexes and learning in general, along with the supposed structural changes, a very important role must be played by metabolic processes. With each new pairing there occurs anew the synthesis of ribonucleic acid (RNA), i.e., intermediary and ribosomal RNA, and also the formation of active protein in postsynaptic regions of association neurons, i.e., a change occurs which takes place upon the first perception of the object of vital importance. Hydén (1965) showed that in rats the quantity of RNA in motor cells is increased after prolonged movement (i.e., swimming) to the point of exhaustion. The increased quantity of RNA is observed even after cessation of the motor activity. It increases over the course of 5 hr and then decreases in 22 hr to normal. Much the same is observed in rats during training to climb along a trellis of stretched wires to receive food. But, in addition, the structure of the RNA changes: the adenyl increases and the uracil decreases. In both cases, the quantity of protein also increases. In this case, these changes disappear in 24 hr.

In general, the accumulation of RNA occurs each time prolonged activity occurs, even if the latter is not related to learning. Thus, Morrell (1961) showed that in rabbits, cats, and monkeys, when some region of the cortex undergoes an increase of activity for a period of several days or weeks as a result of continuous arrival of impulses from some focus of convulsive excitation induced by poisoning with ethyl chloride, then in this region of the cortex the cytoplasm of the pyramidal cells and the initial segment of dendrites become enriched with RNA.

It is characteristic that in the region of continuous activity, bilobate nuclei are observed, which are precursors of cell division. The principal organizing substance in the nucleus of the cell is considered to be deoxyribonucleic acid (DNA), which is related to the synthesis of informational RNA. From this it follows that bilobate nuclei must signify an increase in the quantity of DNA and this in turn must lead to an increased quantity of RNA. The accumulation of this RNA is especially noticeable, according to Morrell, in the cytoplasm adjacent to the cell membrane, i.e., in the postsynaptic regions. Such accumulation of RNA must originate upon formation of a conditioned reflex in the nerve cells related to temporary connections, as a consequence of multiple pairings of conditional and unconditional stimuli. This finding must be of great functional significance, since the accumulation of RNA in the cytoplasm leads to an accumulation of active protein which in turn would affect enzymatic activity and permeability of the postsynaptic membranes and also would favor the activation of the corresponding neural circuits. This chemical shift would undoubtedly play an essential role in the process of training in the form of fixation of the trained activity for a long period of time.

On the other hand, it is very clear from these experiments that the accumulation of RNA in response to prolonged excitation of cells is not of specific significance. It cannot be ruled out that in the activation of the existing potential synapses or the formation of new synapses not only RNA takes part but also other compounds, e.g., phospholipids and other compounds which are necessary for stimulation or for retention of changes in the structure of the active protein. In this way, the active operation of these substances can be reflected both in the biosynthesis, and in the molecular reorganization of protein (Barondes, 1965).

As has previously been pointed out, a conditional stimulus directly activates certain association neurons and then *via* projection pyramidal neurons evokes the external response, e.g., feeding behavior in the form of running to the feeder. This means that the conditional stimulus can lead to the outward response without reproduction of the image of the location of food. Normally, of course, the reproduction of this image is unavoidable. This becomes quite apparent if the unconditional stimulus is altered from the usual environment for the particular behavior. For example, let us suppose that in response to the conditional sound, the dog runs out of the cage to a specific feeder which is located to the right at a distance of 4 m. If the dog is led through a corridor into another room and there settles down in the cage, and then the conditional sound is presented, the dog initially runs out of the cage to the right for 1 to 2 m, as it does in the usual experimental room, but then it stops for a second and quickly turns and runs across the corridor into the experimental room directly to the feeder that had been signaled. It is evident that the direct running to the right is a reflection of the conditioned reflex feeding behavior and that the entire subsequent orienting movement is a reflection of image behavior which ensues as a result of the reproduction of the image of the location of food.

However, under certain pathological conditions the conditioned feeding response can occur even without the reproduction of the image of the place of food. This, for example, is the case with contusion of the brain of the animal as a result of a blast. Automatized conditioned reflex behavior is is retained, but psychoneural memory disappears, so that the animal is unable to go spontaneously to a place where a minute previously it had seen and eaten food (Beritashvili, 1945; Bregadze, 1945). Evidently, the air shock waves, like many other noxious agents, traumatize the sensory stellate elements more strongly then the pyramidal neurons.

Thus, *with multiple repetition of one and the same behavior, long-term memory, in relation to the learned activity, is manifest both on the basis of the development of synaptic structures in association neurons forming temporary connections, and also on the basis of the accumulation of active protein in the postsynaptic portions of the same association neurons.*

Structural and Molecular–Submolecular Changes in the Absence of Training. All of the above-mentioned structural and molecular–submolecular changes with training of a specific activity depend quantitatively on practice, i.e., on rather frequent repetition of the particular trained activity. Therefore, in the absence of practice, these changes gradually become erased, and the reverse development of the structure of synapses occurs: shriveling of the neural terminations, decrease in their number, and also decrease of active protein in the association neurons of the neocortex which facilitate the activity of these synaptic structures. From this it is clear that in the absence of practice the conditioned reflex becomes extinguished, the trained instrumental movement is forgotten, and the image of the object of vital importance ceases to be reproduced in response to the conditional signal.

But the molecular alteration of cytoplasmic protein, with the formation of active protein in the neocortex with prolonged training, becomes sufficiently consolidated and stable that the trained movement can easily be reproduced in unchanged form for years, even for a lifetime, despite infrequent practice.

In this way, presumably, the rapid restoration of conditional feeding behavior that had been extinguished as a consequence of a very prolonged interruption can be explained, even though only a single feeding had occurred under the given conditional signal. Thus, a subsequent evocation of the feeding behavior in response to the conditional signal presumably originates not as a result of a momentary structural development of temporary connections but because the new feeding leads to an increase in the quantity of existing active protein in the association neurons of the neural circuits which were excited by the new perception of food. Therefore, the subsequent trials of the conditional signal presumably evoke the appropriate response as a result of the reproduction of the image of the location of food.

Thus, *when learned behavior, instrumental or conditioned-reflex, is not repeated for a prolonged time interval, synaptic structures in the temporary connections undergo reverse development as to quantity and myelinization of presynaptic endings and also satellite glia. Therefore, at a particular moment, the learned activity ceases to be evoked.* Simultaneously, the active protein accumulated in the postsynaptic regions as a result of metabolism gradually undergoes degradation. As a consequence of the latter, image memory, i.e., the location of the food or the noxious agent, for the learned activity ceases to appear. *If, after a single pairing of the conditional and unconditional stimuli, i.e., feeding or electrical stimulation, the learned activity is restored, then this originates as a consequence of new formation of active protein and the reproduction of the image of the location of the unconditional stimulus, and not from the restoration of the synaptic structures in the temporary connections.*

Delayed Feeding Responses to Conditional Stimuli. As has already been pointed out, the image of the food object perceived by vision or hearing is retained for many minutes after direct perception of it. This also characterizes the image of the place of food which is reproduced by the action of the conditional auditory or visual feeding signal. If the dog is in a closed cage when the latter signal is presented, and the cage is opened after some time has passed, the animal nonetheless runs to the feeder that had been signaled. It has been established that the maximum delay is 10 to 15 min.

It is not difficult to demonstrate that this delayed running, many minutes following the perception of the feeding signal, is not a conditioned reflex. If after presentation of the conditional signal, the dog is taken out of the cage for a few minutes, and led by the collar about the room, and even if it is fed during this time, the appearance of the delayed response is not interfered with. After release, the dog runs in just the same manner to the place of food. Here it must be kept in mind that the delayed response appears even for a conditional stimulus which during the elaboration of the corresponding conditioned reflex was always coincident with an unconditional stimulus, i.e., when the concurrent conditioned reflex was elaborated to the particular conditioned stimulus. If the conditional stimulus is given at the time when the dog is inside the closed cage, the animal gets up and will attempt to go out of the cage. If the stimulation ceases, the animal quiets down. This attempt to leave the cage expresses all of the activity of the temporary connections that had been elaborated, and which characterizes the reflex. If upon opening the cage several minutes after the signal ceases, the dog nonetheless runs to the feeder, despite the fact that prior to release it had been led about the room and fed in an unaccustomed location, then this must of course be recognized not as a manifestation of a conditioned reflex, but as a psychoneural act arising as a consequence of the reproduction of the image of the location of the feeder.

Those neurophysiological processes such as the perception of the food object even after a single repetition are based on delayed responses to conditional stimuli. Initially, delayed responses ensue as a result of reverberation of excitation in temporary connections. This reverberation of excitation is quite apparent in the change of electrical activity of the cortex. According to observations of Oniani and Ordzhonikidze (1968), after the formation of a conditioned reflex of feeding movement by the method of free movement, the conditional signal evokes a desynchronization of the electrical activity in the neocortex and in other extensive structures in the cerebrum. On the other hand, in some structures of the limbic system, distinctive activity in the form of bursts of slow-wave spindles of a frequency of 35 to 40 per sec appears in the amygdala, and a theta rhythm arises in the hippo-

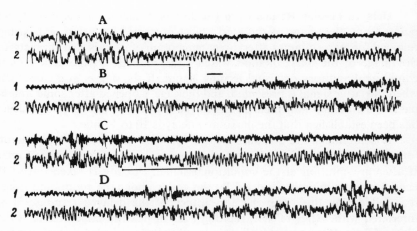

Fig. 12. Changes of background electrical activity of the auditory cortex (1) and in the hippocampus (2) in response to a conditional auditory signal (a 200-cycle tone) which evokes feeding behavior in a cat. A—effect of the conditional signal at the time of a consolidated conditioned reflex; B—termination of this effect 1 min after presentation of the conditional signal; C—effect of the conditional signal, before the consolidation of the conditioned reflex (i.e., after 10 pairings with feeding); D—continuation of record C. Presentation of the conditional signal is denoted by the straight line. Calibration: 100 mV and 1 sec. (Oniani, 1968)

campus (Fig. 12). This altered activity persists after scores of feedings, i.e., before the consolidation of the conditioned reflex, for some 20 to 30 sec (oscillogram C and D in Fig. 12), and after consolidation, for a minute (oscillogram A and B). At this time, the cat is in a waiting, expectant position which is evoked by the image of the feeder signaled, which is in turn evoked by the conditional stimulus, and then is retained for the entire time of the altered electrical activity, i.e., the reverberation of excitation in the temporary connections.

It is characteristic that the desynchronization of electrical activity in the neocortex disappears somewhat earlier than the expectant stance of the animal, the electrical spindles of a rhythm of 35 to 40 per sec, and the theta rhythm in the paleocortex.

The disappearance of the desynchronization of the electrical activity in the neocortex which is evoked by the conditional signal is presumably related to the cessation of reverberation of excitation in neuronal circuits of the neocortex. Correspondingly, there must be, on one hand, a cessation of the activation of sensory elements of the cortex, as a consequence of which the image of the location of the signaled feeder disappears, and, on the other hand, the excitation of efferent pathways from the neocortex to the paleocortex and subcortical structures presumably ceases, and correspondingly, the expectant stance of the animal, the electrical slow-wave spindles, and the theta rhythm in the paleocortex disappear.

Upon cessation of the reverberation of excitation, the animals settle down, lower the heads, and lie down with the heads to one side or the other. But after several minutes, as was indicated previously, the animals will go to the feeder that had been signaled if the door of the room in which the dog is located is open. This short-term memory is dependent on the fact that during the reverberation of excitation, a large quantity of synaptic vesicles is formed, vesicles which secrete the active substance or mediator entering the synaptic regions. Moreover, active protein accumulates in the postsynaptic regions which is presumably formed by participation of RNA. Acting upon the postsynaptic membrane, this protein facilitates transmission of excitation. As a result of all of this, the reverberation of excitation in the neuronal circuits can be produced anew if there is some change in the environment, e.g., upon opening the door of the room in which the animal is located. In this connection, the reproduction of the image of the corresponding feeder occurs, and the animal goes to it in accordance with this image.

After conditioned feeding behavior to a specific feeder is formed, the animal attempts to approach it, not only during the presentation of the conditional signal or several minutes afterwards, but even independently, for example, when the animal is brought into the experimental room at the beginning of an experimental day. The same even occurs many days after the last feeding. Such long-term memory of the animal is determined by activation of association neuronal circuits in which the excitation had been increased as a result of the facilitating action of the specific protein-activator retained in them. Moreover, impulses originating from these neurons, via their collaterals, activate sensory stellate neurons (which reproduce the image of the location of food), and also the specific projectional neurons which give rise to the turning of the head, the eyes, and the subsequent movement in the direction of the feeder.

The Neural Mechanism of Formation of Trace- or Successive Conditioned Reflex. In Pavlov's laboratory, the formation of a special type of delayed reflex termed the trace-conditioned reflex was studied in detail. The feeding was carried out after a 1 to 2 min interval following cessation of the conditioning signal (Dobrovol'skii, 1911; Grossman, 1910). Delayed defensive reflexes of the extremity, formed by means of adding an unconditional electrical stimulus some time after the conditional signal, were also studied (Beritashvili, 1925). After a series of pairings, the unconditioned reflex initially appeared from the very beginning of the conditional stimulus, i.e., it was coincident with the latter. Later it became delayed, at times appearing during the stimulation, at times following it. Still later it appeared mainly after stimulation. Such a conditioned reflex, which I termed successive, can be formed only upon presenting the basic stimulus not more than 1 to 2 min after the conditional stimulus. The shorter the interval between the conditional and the basic stimulus, the more rapidly such a successive reflex appears. A hundred pairings are necessary for the reflex to become more or less consolidated, and it is quickly extinguished without reinforcement.

Such delayed conditioned responses cannot be considered to be manifestations of memory. They are elaborated with great difficulty; if the unconditional stimulus follows the conditional stimulus by more than 1 to 2 min, the latter is unable to influence the association pyramidal neurons which are excited by the unconditional stimulus to the degree that synaptic connections are developed on them from axons of the association pyramidal neurons that are excited by the conditional stimulus. Such development can only occur if these axons continue to be excited until the moment of the unconditional stimulus, i.e., up to the moment of increased excitability in the association neurons which are excited by the unconditional stimulus. But an interval of 1 to 2 min is sufficiently long, so that neurons of the circuit excited by the conditional stimulus cease to have an increased excitability up to the moment of the occurrence of the unconditional stimulus. A score of pairings of the conditional and the unconditional stimuli are necessary to increase the persistence of activity in the neural circuits of the conditional stimulus so that they can act upon the association neurons which are excited by the unconditional stimulus. In this way, a feed-forward temporary connection arises. The advent of the coincident conditioned reflex is linked to this moment.

For this conditioned reflex to be reinforced, it is necessary to form an inverse connection, i.e., in order for the association pyramidal neurons excited by the unconditional stimulus to influence those neurons which are excited by the conditional stimulus. This cannot be the case upon the first pairing, for the excitability in the association neurons of the conditional stimulus diminishes somewhat in the course of the 1 to 2 min until the occurrence of the unconditional stimulus, so that the association neurons of the unconditional stimulus cannot act on those of the conditional stimulus. However, this can occur if the conditional stimulus is sufficiently strong and is repeated some 10 times in combination with the unconditional stimulus. Only under these conditions do inverse temporary connections arise as a result of the development of synaptic structures on the association pyramidal cells which are excited by the conditional stimulus. Together with the formation and strengthening of inverse connections, a strengthened and prolonged circulation of excitation in these directional temporary connections takes place. This is related to an increase in the generalized inhibition of the cortex which results from the activation of the mass of dendrites by the collaterals from neuronal circuits of the temporary connections. This generalized inhibition impedes the advent of the concurrent conditioned reflex. Only when the inverse temporary connections become fatigued, which occurs earlier than the fatigue of the more developed successive temporary connections, does the generalized inhibition diminish, and then the conditioned reflex can appear.

But the more strongly the inverse connections are developed, the longer will the excitation circulate in the neuronal circuits of the temporary connections. This can occur not only during the conditional stimulus, but even after it. Accordingly, the conditioned reflex can appear in connection with fatigue of the inverse connections, not only during the conditional stimulus, but even after it, in such a way that the later the inverse connections become fatigued, the later the generalized inhibitory effect diminishes.

It must be presumed that during the formation of a trace-conditioned reflex, the image of the conditional (sound) and the unconditional (the location of the food or the noxious agent) arises immediately upon the first perception of them. But in view of the large interval between them (1 to 2 min), the sensory elements they excite are not connected in a single functional system. As a result, the conditional stimulus cannot evoke the image of the location of food nor the noxious agent and thus determine the appearance of the corresponding behavior.

But, presumably, after many scores of pairings with the formation of temporary connections, such a functional system is established, owing to the fact that association pyramidal neurons of the temporary connections, by means of their collaterals, establish a connection with the sensory neurons which are excited by the conditional and unconditional stimuli. From this moment the reproduction of the image of the location of food or of the noxious agent can participate in evoking of the conditioned response.

Simultaneously, with the development of synaptic structures of temporary connections, RNA-mediator and active protein accumulate in the postsynaptic regions. This facilitates not only the appearance of the conditioned reflex immediately after the conditional signal, but also upon repetition of the conditional signal in the following days.

However, in children trace or successive responses with an interval of 1 to 2 min are acquired somewhat more rapidly than in dogs, i.e., even after the very first pairing of the indifferent stimulus with the conditional one (putting chocolate in their mouth). These responses are more stable and less sensitive to extraneous stimulation (Leonov, 1926). But in children these individually acquired responses are not conditioned; they occur in accordance with the image of food, i.e., on the basis of image memory. Only after multiple successive pairings can the indifferent stimulus become conditional, i.e., evoke the feeding response through temporary connections. This means that in man the capability of connecting two different influences of the external world into a single functional system is somewhat greater than in the dog, for such a union is accomplished in the first instance by psychoneural activity.

Thus, *in the dog, the capability of connection of an indifferent stimulus with an unconditional one separated from one another by an interval of 1 to 2 min is not very great. This is related to the greater difficulty of its implementation by means of development of temporary connections. Under the some conditions, the connection of the images of the indifferent and unconditional stimuli are also impeded. Evidently, this connection becomes manifest for the first time when the temporary connection between them has become established.*

In children, the capability of formation of connections between an indifferent stimulus and a subsequent unconditional one is significantly higher. In children, such connections can appear after the very first trial, because of strongly developed image psychoneural activity.

Conditioned Reflex Memory in the Archipaleocortex. As is known, in decorticate animals, a conditioned feeding reflex to sound and light is formed only after a large number of pairings (Ten Cate, 1934; Belenkov, 1965). The ability to form conditioned reflexes disappears in mammals only after removal of the entire cortex, together with the basal ganglia (Zelenyi, 1911–1912, 1930; Popov, 1953).

It should be noted that in normal animals, temporary connections between a conditional and an unconditional stimulus must arise simultaneously both in the new and the old cortex. As a basis of this can be cited first the fact that an unconditioned feeding or defensive reflex is evoked by local stimulation of the old cortex and is always associated with the appearance of the corresponding emotional excitation; secondly, stimulation of any receptor evokes electrical potentials, i.e., produces an excitation of neurons not only in the new cortex but also in almost all parts of the old, and thirdly, the emotional response evoked by stimulation of the old cortex can easily be related to any particular stimulus. From this it is clear why feeding behavior and defensive conditioned reflexes can arise both *via* the new and *via* the old cortex, in response to stimulation of any particular receptor (Beritashvili, 1963).

However, the structural changes that are produced in the association neurons of the old cortex upon the formation of a conditioned reflex are presumably very insignificant and very unstable, for conditioned reflexes are not reinforced to such a degree that they are evoked with great regularity and retained without practice for many days. It is characteristic that in animals devoid of the neocortex, conditional feeding signals produce an appropriate response only during the signal, and as soon as the signal ceases, the conditioned feeding response also disappears. This evidently occurs as a result of the fact that in such animals temporary connections are developed in the paleocortex between neurons perceiving the conditional stimulus and the integrative mechanism of the unconditioned feeding behavior, and these connections exist mainly as directed from the neuronal complex for the conditional stimulus to the integrative mechanism for feeding behavior (forward connection). In general, it is known that even in the neocortex inverse connections are developed later and more weakly than ones in the forward direction (Beritashvili, 1932). It is evident that in the old cortex this ability is especially strong; therefore, in the old cortex reverberation in the temporary neural circuits cannot last long enough to result in a prolonged reflex after-effect. It is probable that this also explains the fact that conditioned movement toward the place of food ceases immediately after termination of the conditional stimulus.

According to our experiments, in cats without a neocortex, a conditioned reflex movement towards a feeder in response to a specific sound or light stimulus is elaborated during the presence of the signal at the feeder after many feedings; this conditioned movement is unstable and is not fully differentiated, but it is retained for many days. This means that conditioned reflex memory is intrinsic in animals deprived of the neocortex. Thus, if the signal is transferred to another place after formation of the reflex, the cat does not go to the feeder but to the signal; it approaches the latter and begins to sniff at it. Further, it is known that if the animal is kept in the cage during the feeding signal and is released 2 to 5 sec later, it does not go directly to the place of food. Or, if the conditional signal ceases during the movement of the animal to the feeder, the cat then loses its orientation and begins to wander about the room (Nutsubidze and Ordzhonikidze, 1961; Kvirtsk-haliya, 1967).

From such observations, it follows that, in cats without a neocortex, conditioned reflex movement toward the feeder under the conditions mention-ed is directly related to the orienting response of the head to the particular signal. When the animal is fed, after being led to the feeder while the con-ditional sound signal is being presented, neural connections with the motor centers of the orienting response of the head are strongly developed in the limbic system. It is clear that orienting movement of the head ensues in response to the isolated effect of the auditory signal, and the animal goes in the direction of the sound to which the head is turned.

If the conditional signal ceases, a cat without the neocortex does not go to the feeder that had been signaled. This presumably occurs because, as was indicated previously, such a cat is deprived of psychoneural image memory. Therefore, in response to the conditional signal, image of the location of the feeder which would direct the animal to the place of feeding after the cessation of the conditional signal does not arise. It is true that in neuronal circuits of the paleocortex, reverberation of excitation also occurs, but as a result of the insufficient development of temporary connections, the reverberation necessarily ceases when the conditional signal is terminated.

In a cat without the neocortex, conditioned reflex movement to the feeder can also be elaborated during a conditional signal at a distance from the feeding place. In this case, many reinforcements from the given feeder are required, such that the cat will go to the feeder if the signal is terminated before opening the cage. We suppose that in this case the conditional signal and the opening of the cage evoke only an exit from the cage. Motion toward the feeder, presumably, results from the formation of a chain conditioned reflex such that labyrinthine and proprioceptive stimuli occurring during each segment of the behavior are transformed into conditional signals for the following segment of it.

But even under these conditions the animal without a neocortex cannot go directly to the feeder even after some seconds following termination of the signal and the opening of the cage, since it cannot reproduce the image of the location of food under the influence of the environment because of the absence of image memory.

In general, it is known that cats without a neocortex are unable, following a single feeding or even after multiple feedings from a specific feeder, to run to it spontaneously either after several seconds following feeding or on the next day. From this experiment it is quite evident that cats without the neocortex do not have the capability of image activity, and also cannot even project into space an image of the feeder from which they had received food tens or hundreds of times (Ordzhonikidze and Nutsubidze, 1961). From this it follows that during perception of the external world, the same intracellular molecular processes which can lead to the origin of RNA-intermediary for formation of active protein do not occur in the association neurons of the paleocortex. Therefore, one can say that the paleocortex cannot serve as the basis for either short-term or long-term image memory.

As was pointed out previously, according to our observations, memory for the emotional response of fear is long-term. This expression of memory presumably depends upon features of the association neurons connecting sensory neurons of fear with association neurons of the paleocortex which are excited by the external world during the experience of fear. It is evident that stable active protein is formed immediately in these association neurons upon the first excitation and then, with fear, any indifferent stimulus exciting the neocortex is related to these sensory neurons from the very first time *via* association neurons. From this it follows that *indifferent stimuli, upon repetition, can evoke a fully developed emotional response, owing to the fact that the association neurons excited by such stimuli, which interconnect sensory neurons of fear, are presumably connected via an innate pathway with the corresponding integrating mechanism of the emotional behavior.*

Thus, conditioned feeding reflexes in an animal without a neocortex are formed to sound after some tens of feedings, if the source of the sound is located at the feeder from which the animal is fed, and after many tens of feedings, if the source of the sound is located elsewhere. In the first instance, temporary connections are elaborated with the orienting movement of the head, which directs the movement of the animal to the source of the sound. In the second case, a chain conditioned reflex of movement toward the cage is formed in response to proprioceptive and labyrinthine stimulation. These temporary connections are very weakly developed, although they can be activated by a conditional signal even after many days, and thereby reflect conditioned reflex memory. But the reverberation of excitation evidently occurs only during the signal, and the excitability is increased thereby only very insignificantly; it is therefore impossible to evoke a delayed response to the conditional signal.

MEMORY IN MAN

All of the phenomena of memory described above, i.e., image, conditioned reflex, and emotional, are also characteristic of man. It can be asserted that at an early age children possess all of these aspects of memory, and their behavior is exclusively regulated by them. Only with age, when children begin to speak and reason, and when the representation of the external world and of internal conditions is retained in verbal symbols, does a new form of memory, which can be termed verbal–logical, begin to take place in man. This form of memory is evidently fundamentally related to the extraordinary development of the cerebral cortex.

We have good evidence for this supposition. Beritashvili and Dzidzishvili (1934) studied the behavior of a microcephalic girl, who represented a unique state of microcephaly, i.e., an extreme underdevelopment of the cerebral cortex. The girl had been brought into the psychiatric clinic from the street by a policeman, and lived there for three years. It was decided by the anatomist, A. A. Natishvili, that she was about 10 years old. All of her sensory receptors were developed normally, but she could not speak and did not understand speech; she articulated only meaningless sounds and did not understand the significance of different types of human behavior. Emotionally she was readily excitable, uncontrollably aggressive, and she scratched, bit, and cried out with an inhuman voice. We called this girl Pita, from the name of our forebear, Pithecanthropus. Pita did not dress herself, could not sweep the room, and did not know how to use a stick so as to bring to herself a piece of food situated beyond a grating; if we placed food on the table and covered it with a bowl, she did not know how to get it out from under the bowl, but if we showed food from behind some obstacle, and then led her to that place, she remembered it and as soon as she was released, she would run to the place of food. This means that in this girl there was image memory and that behavior was regulated by images.

On the basis of Pita's image behavior, automatized instrumental motion was easily established. For example, she taught herself how to use a stick for bringing food closer in the same way that monkeys did in the experiments of Köhler (1921). Some sticks of different lengths were placed in front of the grating and food was placed at various distances behind the screen. If the food was close, she used her hand to obtain the food through the grating, but if the food was located farther away, she did not attempt to take the stick to bring the food closer. When the experimenter put one of the sticks in Pita's hand, she began to swing it pointlessly in front of the grating. Afterwards, she took first one, then another stick, but she simply amused herself with them. Then the experimenter, in front of her, pushed the stick through the grating and moved the food. Pita, stretched out her hand and, immediately secured the food. Despite such help from the experimenter, Pita never made use of the stick when the experiment was repeated and continued to amuse herself in front of the grating. Only after three repetitions of the same manipulation by the experimenter did Pita push the stick through the grating in an imitative manner, but she did not begin to move the food. The experimenter gave her still more help: he took her hand, in which she held the stick, and helped her extend the stick to the food and moved it toward the grating. This manipulation was repeated by the experimenter in the following trial. After this trial, Pita used the stick each time for bringing a distant object nearer.

From these observations it clearly follows that Pita, like animals, could carry out a specific goal-directed instrumental behavior while she had the image of the given movement. In this experiment with a stick, the image arose only when she reached for the reward with the aid of the stick by her own movement. In the establishment of this motor image, proprioceptive stimulation of the hand participates, together with the visual receptors. It is characteristic that she took a stick of any length; if the latter was short, and the reward could not be reached, Pita threw it away and took another stick, sometimes an even shorter one. Consequently, she did not distinguish sticks from a "functional" standpoint. This means that upon seeing the food and the stick, a motor image arose in Pita of bringing the food nearer by means of the stick, but there was no conscious relationship to this behavior.

After many repetitions, this image instrumental movement became automatic, and a chain of conditioned reflexes arose: Temporary connections were formed between the sight of the stick and the motion of the hand for grasping it, then between the musculocutaneous stimulation upon taking the stick in the hand and the subsequent extending it in the direction of the food, between the view of grasping the food with the stick and the subsequent motion of the stick by which the food is brought closer, and finally between the view of the food at a closer distance and the grasping of the food by the hand. Once formed, such a chain of conditioned reflexes was retained for many days or months, and in this way was expressed as conditioned-reflex memory arising on the basis of image behavior.

Conditioned-reflex memory in Pita appeared in many instrumental habits which she elaborated on the basis of imitative or random goal-directed behavior. When we began to form conditioned feeding behavior in her, we noticed that if, within her view, food was placed under a bowl, she was not able to obtain the latter. However, in response to a signal (a bell), Pita would usually go to a specific location of food, and finding food on a plate there, she would eat it.

In one instance, in Pita's presence, food was placed not on the plate but under an inverted plate, and then Pita was immediately led away. After three minutes, in response to the conditional signal, Pita went up to the usual location of food, but not finding it on the plate, stood still, completely helpless, and did not even touch the plate. Upon repetition of this experiment on the following day, and even after six months, she was unsuccessful. It was of course necessary to teach her to obtain the food from underneath the plate. We repeated this experiment after a year. It was found that as a result of spontaneous activities in the clinic, she learned to obtain the food from underneath the plate if she saw that it had been placed there.

After a year of living in the clinic, Pita had noticeably changed. She became somewhat more gentle, more friendly to the attendant personnel, and even showed some empathy for certain people. She responded appropriately to some commands: close the door, come here, move away, open the faucet, greet the doctor, and wipe the nose. Such types of responses to verbal commands can also be elaborated in the dog: It will run to a feeder on the complex command: "to the feeder"; it will run to another feeder on the right to the command: "to the right", and it will go to its own place upon the command: "to your place", and so on. Pita attempted to put on clothes, but having forced the head into a blouse, she could not get the arms into the sleeves. However, the main point was that Pita gradually began to show many different instrumental movements in the form of working habits. They presumably appeared on the basis of strongly developed imitability. She imitated simple working movements of the employees: washing her face under the faucet, feeling the pulse of patients, removing dishes from the table, sweeping the floor, drying the floor with a mop, and so on. All of these instrumental movements did not extend beyond pure mimicry. The very essence or thought of acts of work remained elusive for Pita, i.e., they were subconscious. All of these imitative movements were elaborated on the basis of visual and movement images after one or several random mimicking movements, and then were reinforced as a result of multiple repetitions, as a result of the formation of temporary connections.

Following the death of this 13-year-old girl, it was found that the cerebral hemispheres were of the weight of those of the chimpanzee, the cortical gyri were like those of a chimpanzee or somewhat less than in a newborn infant. The total cortical surface was 4.3 times smaller than that of a 10-year-old child. Consequently, in Pita, the cerebral cortex did not have the postembryonic development that is characteristic for the brain of man; it was typical of that for a chimpanzee.

Despite this cortical defect in Pita, all of the sensory receptors functioned normally. She used the hands like a normal adult person and possessed all of the human emotions. She conducted her behavior and her acclimatization to the conditions of life on the basis of image and conditioned-reflex memory, like a young child. She did not have the complex-logical memory that is specific for man. Therefore, it must be concluded that *complex-logical memory is organically related to extremely large postembryonic development of the cortex of the cerebral hemispheres. On the other hand, although complex-logical memory in the normal human adult predominates, he conducts himself in his behavior to a significant degree according to image, emotional, and conditioned-reflex memory.*

PHYLOGENETIC DEVELOPMENT OF MEMORY

Heretofore, we have expounded mainly on memory on the basis of experiments with the behavior of dogs, and to some degree we have also studied it in all types of vertebrates, from fish to monkeys. In this work, all aspects of memory were studied: image, emotional, and conditioned-reflex. We employed the same method of free movement. Since study of memory is possible only on animals that are well accustomed to the experimental environment, to the same experimenter, and to all of his procedures, it was necessary to accustom the animals these experimental conditions for greater or lesser periods of time.

In all of these types of animals, we studied memory in relation to the location of food after a single perception of it in a new location, in relation to the place of food following many perceptions of it, in a given location in response to the same signal, and also in relation to the location of painful stimulation after a single experience with the latter.

In all of these cases, the different aspects of memory were studied in the same manner, which was approximately the same as that for dogs. The animal was shown food at a distance or was led to the place of food and allowed to eat, and then was returned to its accustomed, enclosed abode. After different intervals of time, the animal was released and its behavior observed. If the animal went directly to the place of food, we considered this response a manifestation of image memory. If the animal, after painful electrical stimulation at a specific place, ran away from that place or resisted forcibly being led to it, we considered this a manifestation of emotional memory. Conditioned-reflex memory was also studied in relation to prolonged retention of a conditioned reflex, following its formation.

Until recently, we studied behavior in those forms of animals in which the neocortex is developed to a greater or lesser degree (rabbits, cats, dogs). As was pointed out previously, sensations of different modalities (visual, auditory, etc.) were produced by activation of sensory stellate neurons from pericellular axonal nets in layers III and IV of the primary area of the perceiving region stimulated by afferent impulses. The retention of the perceived object in the form of an image, i.e., memory for this object, depends in the first instance on integrated activity of association neurons of the secondary areas, which integrate stellate and pyramidal neurons of the primary area activated by the given object. Therefore, it must be presumed that image behavior, as well as image memory, must be rudimentary in such lower forms as reptiles, in which the cortex is very slightly developed, and even less so in fish and amphibia, in which the cortex is generally absent.

On the other hand, in lower vertebrates there are undoubtedly sensory elements in the brain which give rise to the sensations from the environment that are perceived *via* the receptors. They also have association neurons which integrate the sensory elements thus producing the perception of concrete objects. We know very well that these animals—fish, amphibia, and reptiles—not only perceive external objects, but correctly project their location into the environment, and this enables them to develop appropriate movements in relation to the objects perceived, i.e., to adapt to the conditions of the environment.

The question of whether images of the environment are formed in these animals, how long they are retained in memory, and the nature of their retention, had not been studied experimentally until recently.

Under the influence of study of conditioned reflexes in dogs, many authors carried out analogous experiments on lower vertebrates, such as fish (Frolov, 1926; Malyukina, 1955; Karamyan, 1956), amphibia (Beritashvili, 1929; Leutskii, 1929; Beburishvili and Chichinadze, 1936), turtles (Polyakov, 1930), and lizards (Diebschlag, 1934, 1938; Wagner, 1933, and others). The purpose of all of these authors was to establish how quickly a feeding or defensive conditioned reflex could be elaborated, and how quickly they could be differentiated to artificial sound or light stimuli.

Only in recent years in the Physiological Laboratory of Tbilisi State University has the specific aim been set to study all of these animals, with the purpose of bringing out their image memory as well as emotional and conditioned-reflex memory, and in this way to reveal the level of development of memory in its phylogenetic aspect in these forms.

In lower vertebrates, the experiments were carried out on fish (goldfish), amphibia (frogs), and reptiles (turtles and lizards).

Memory in Fish. The experiments on fish were carried out by N. Sikharulidze (1967) in an aquarium 1 m long and 50 cm wide. It was divided crosswise into three sections. One section of the aquarium of 20 cm length was divided off by a movable transparent partition. The fish under study were usually placed here in pairs. The opposite end of the aquarium was divided into three sections by means of opaque partitions. Here, in one of the sections, food was offered. The fish had to swim through the middle portion of 60 cm length in order to reach the food.

The experiments were conducted as follows: The transverse partition was raised and, with the aid of a cheesecloth net, fish were driven into one of the sections where they were given food. After eating, the fish were returned to their usual living place by means of the same net, and the partition was lowered. Initially the fish were very frightened by this procedure and scattered about. But gradually they became accustomed to it, and began to follow the net of their own accord. Later, the fish were released some time after feeding by raising the partition. It was found that if this interval was not more than 8 to 10 sec, the fish immediately swam directly to the section where they had been fed. After a longer interval, however, they usually swam in the middle portion of the aquarium and remained there.

Emotional Memory in Fish. Fish were trained to receive food in a specific location, and they were always found in the location where they had customarily received food. In the same place, electrodes for painful stimulation were introduced. If electrical stimulation was carried out during feeding on one occasion, the fish immediately swam away from this location, but after 10 to 12 sec they swam up to it anew and began to eat. This means that in this case the location of painful stimulation had a negative effect on the fish which was somewhat more prolonged than the positive action of the place of feeding. This negative influence on the fish must be considered a manifestation of emotional memory.

Conditioned-Reflex Memory in Fish. The rapidity with which conditional feeding behavior could be formed and the duration of retention of it were also studied. In general, it is known that in fish a conditioned feeding reflex to sound and to light can be formed relatively rapidly, e.g., after 3 to 5 pairings, according to Frolov (1926). But in experiments carried out by N.

Sikharulidze (1967) on goldfish, conditioned feeding reflexes were formed after an appreciably longer period of time. These experiments were carried out in the following manner: Initially, the partition was raised during the conditional sound, and the net directed the fish to the place of food in one of the sections. At this point the sound was terminated. After eating, the fish were returned to their usual place by means of the net. After 14 to 24 feedings, it was sufficient to present the signal and to raise the partition to have the fish swim to the place of food unprompted. Nor was it always necessary to use the net for the return course. Tapping the wall of the aquarium or agitating the water by touching the screen was sufficient for the fish to swim back to their accustomed place.

Conditioned feeding behavior was also elaborated to a red light. If from time to time a yellow light was used and the fish were not taken to the feeder, then after repeated trials the fish ceased to respond to the yellow light. However, this differentiation was not stable.

After multiple feedings with the red signal, the conditioned-reflex movement became reinforced to the degree that it appeared after a prolonged interruption in the work. It could be evoked by the signal upon the first presentation of the latter after two weeks or even after two months following a few pairings.

This means that in fish, feeding behavior to the image of a location of food which had been perceived on a single occasion is retained for 8 to 10 sec altogether, and that conditioned-reflex behavior resulting from morphological development of temporary connections is retained for many days.

After a conditioned reflex had become highly stabilized in the fish, we began to investigate how long the active influence of the conditioned signal was retained following its cessation. In these cases, the partition was not raised immediately, but some time after the presentation of the signal. It was found that after 8 to 10 sec following the signal, the fish swam up to the place of food that had been signaled. But after a longer interval, they swam about randomly in the aquarium.

If an opaque partition was introduced into the path to the place of food, the fish were initially frightened and swam back, but after a few trials, they went around the obstacle and swam in a goal-directed manner to the place of food. In subsequent experiments, they carried out this avoidance behavior appreciably more rapidly.

Thus, *bony fish* (of the species *Carassius auratus*) *retain the place of feeding or of painful stimulation in memory for only a very short time—not more than 8 to 12 sec.* This means that in this species of fish, the image of the location of food is established immediately after a single feeding, and similarly, the image of the location of painful stimulation after the fish had been subjected to a single occasion of this stimulation. These images are projected and retained in memory for approximately 12 sec. Thus, in correspondence with the image of the presence of food, the fish swims directly to the feeding place for a period of up to 8 to 10 sec, and according to the image of the presence of a painful stimulus, it ceases to swim to this place for a period of 10 to 12 sec. Daily repetition of the experiments did not result in a longer retention of the image, nor prolong the interval of motor activity.

Fish carried out goal-directed avoidance of an obstacle, initially in just the same way as according to the image of the location of food behind the obstacle, but after many repetitions of this path according to the image of the location of food, the avoidance occurs as a conditioned-reflex path.

Thus, it can be said that *bony fish possess memory, i.e., the ability of image and emotional psychoneural activity, in a very rudimentary aspect; reflex memory is more characteristic of them than image or emotional psycho-neural memory.*

The Role of the Forebrain in Memory of Fish. After investigation of image and conditioned-reflex behavior, removal of the forebrain was carried out in fish, the operation being carried out according to the method described by Karamyan (1956) and Kholodov (1963). The forebrain was removed by a transverse section from the remaining brain structures and removed from the cranial vault, the bony defect being restored by application of a liquid mixture of wax and vaseline (2: 1). Observations were carried out on the operated fish for $2\frac{1}{2}$ to 3 months after operation. The results of the operation were subjected to histological control (Sikharulidze, 1967).

The most clear-cut changes in the behavior of the fish were observed in the period of 3 to 4 hr after operation. Initially, they lay immobile on the surface of the water; afterwards they began to swim, rocking from side to side, and turned on their sides. Within 4 or 5 hr after operation, their movements had already become indistinguishable from the movements of normal fish, and they seized food actively.

Toward the end of the same day, the fish were transferred into the experimental aquarium, in which they oriented themselves as usual. A large number of experiments convinced us that conditioned-reflex behavior of the fish had not suffered. Conditioned reflexes which had been elaborated to visual and auditory stimuli were fully retained. Some time (approximately 15 to 18 days) following the operation, disturbed differentiation of conditional light signals (red and yellow light) remained. Still later, the differentiation was restored but it was inexact and unstable. However, it should be noted that in intact fish, differentiation of conditional signals is characteristically unstable.

Following removal of the forebrain, image feeding behavior in fish was severely impaired. Prior to operation, when food had been in a new location, they went directly to this place when they were released after an 8 to 10 sec interval from their usual abode. However, after operation they did not swim to the location of the feeding object which had been perceived, even for a 2 to 3 sec interval after feeding at that location.

After a single electrical stimulation in the new location, intact fish swam away from it. Operated fish, however, would readily swim to a place where they had been stimulated a few (4 to 5) seconds previously.

Moreover, fish ceased to avoid obstacles which were placed in the path to the location of the food object, nor did they show imitative responses.

In this way, we became convinced that *following removal of the forebrain in fish, image behavior is disturbed, whereas conditioned-reflex behavior remains unimpaired.*

We also studied delayed responses to conditional light and sound stimuli following removal of the forebrain. In the period 8 to 10 sec following the signal, normal fish proceeded to the location of the food which had been signaled, whereas after operation, delayed responses to conditional signals were severely impaired. Even 4 or 5 sec after the presentation of the conditional stimulus (both for light and for sound), the fish either did not go out of their usual area or they went in the wrong direction.

From these observations, it incidentally follows that in normal fish, delayed responses after a conditional signal appeared not as a result of the excitatory after-activity of temporary connections, but as a result of the image of the location of food, i.e., image memory.

This means that in fish, all of those sensory and association neurons which upon the very first stimulus are functionally connected among themselves and also with neurons of coordinating motor mechanisms, and can effect an appropriate feeding response for a short time, are located in the forebrain.

It is known that conditioned-reflex activity in fish is especially dependent on the cerebellum. Following its removal, existing conditioned feeding behavior reflexes disappear (Karamyan, 1956). They can be formed anew, but a considerably greater number of feedings (as many as 150 to 200) than in normal fish are necessary. These reflexes are very unstable, often not being evident on the next day. But it is characteristic that, according to a recent experiment by N. Sikharulidze, delayed responses to complex perception of food in a new location are well exhibited, especially after 3 to 4 weeks following the removal of the cerebellum. Moreover, when conditioned reflexes were restored, delayed responses appeared even to conditional stimuli.

Following removal of the cerebellum and the forebrain, both image and conditioned-reflex activity are severely impaired. For restoration of a conditioned feeding-behavior reflex to sound or to light, more than 300 pairings are necessary, and the reflexes are more unstable than following removal of the cerebellum alone. This means that conditioned reflexes can be formed if both the diencephalon and the midbrain remain, but the reflexes are significantly weaker than those formed when the cerebellum is intact (Kholodov, 1963; Sikharulidze, 1968).

Thus, in bony fish, image memory, like memory for the emotion of fear, is brought about by activity of the forebrain. Conditioned-reflex memory, presumably, is a function of the cerebellum and also the diencephalon and midbrain.

Memory in Amphibia. Working at various times of the year on different amphibia (tritons and frogs), we obtained different results. The best results were obtained in our work on frogs in the winter. These frogs were entrapped in the autumn and were placed in a cement pond in an unheated, semi-darkened basement room. They were brought to the experimental room only for experiments, where they remained the entire time until the experiment was completed. The experiments were carried out in the autumn as well as in winter and spring. Surprisingly, these frogs did not take food, not even live worms. We were therefore unable to study their feeding behavior, and hence, memory for the location of food. We were only able to study conditioned defensive behavior and memory for the location of a noxious agent.

When adult frogs or quite young frogs, undergoing the process of metamorphosis, were caught in the late spring and summer, they were brought directly to the laboratory room. Their feeding behavior could be observed and thus image and emotional memory could be studied.

Tritons were brought in the summer and in warm spring days and were kept in aquaria in the laboratory at room temperature. Experiments on defensive and feeding behavior were carried out on them the year around.

Memory in Winter Frogs. On these frogs, the experiments were carried out in a box of dimensions 60 × 60 cm. The box was divided into two sections by means of an opaque partition in which there were openings through which the frogs could move freely from one section to another. On the floor of one of the sections, conductors through which an electrical current could be made to flow were affixed. Frogs, sometimes in a quantity of 3 to 4, were placed in this compartment. When the current was switched on, they began to jump and quickly went over to the other section, whereupon the stimulation was terminated and the frogs quieted down.

If, immediately after this, they were placed again in the conducting section, they did not manifest any restlessness. This procedure was repeated many times with the same result. From these experiments it follows that neither a single nor repeated noxious stimuli in a particular environment evoke avoidance of the environment in the frog; evidently, the particular circumstances of stimulation are not perceived as such, which means that there is no image of the location of the noxious agent in the animal's memory.

Conditioned-Reflex Memory in Amphibia. Using the very same method, we attempted to form conditioned defensive responses to a bell in frogs. We stimulated the frogs a hundred times simultaneously with the bell ringing and by means of an electrical current in the wired portion, and thus compelled them to move to the other section. Despite this, neither the bell nor the conducting section itself became a conditional signal for movement into the other section (Beritashvili, 1929; Sikharulidze, 1967).

We did succeed in forming a conditioned reflex under these circumstances to croaking of another frog, which frogs doubtless perceive. During the croaking evoked from another frog, electrical stimulation of the frog under study was carried out in the wired section. A conditioned reflex to the croaking was elaborated slowly in the frog after 22 to 27 pairings in the month of May, and after 42 to 131 pairings in October. Upon hearing the croaking, the experimental frog moved to the other section. However, this reflex did not become consolidated; it had not become fixed even after 500 to 600 pairings and was not regularly evoked at the beginning of an experimental day. To quite another sound, such as the strokes of a metronome and the sound of an organ pipe, the defensive reflex was not, in general, elaborated (Beritashvili, 1929). But to the light of an electric bulb, the conditioned-defensive reflex under the same circumstances was formed again in a very unstable form after many dozens of pairings (Beburishvili and Chichinadze, 1936).

Conditioned defensive reflexes have been studied in frogs by many authors. Some workers, like us, were not able to form a conditioned reflex to an unusual sound (Leutskii, 1929). Other authors were able to establish defensive reflexes to such sounds (Bianki, 1963, 1967). But under all conditions, these reflexes were very unstable; the conditional sound or light signal sometimes evoked the reflex, sometimes not.

Defensive movements to sound and light are hardly conditioned reflexes. It is well known that, in general, sound has an influence on the central nervous system of the frog. For example, it is known that an unusual sound, which of itself does not evoke movement, reinforces an innate defensive reflex evoked by electrical stimulation of the feet (Beburishvili, 1937). Despite this, conditioned defensive reflexes are not always successfully formed to sound. Frogs most of all form conditioned reflexes to croaking. This, presumably, occurs as a consequence of an increased excitability in the central motor apparatus of the defensive reflex and as the result of a strong physiological effect on this apparatus of the croaking of another frog. Such an interpretation is indicated by the fact that croaking evokes a defensive movement more regularly shortly after pairing with an electrical stimulus, after many seconds, i.e., as long as synaptic potentiation persists. Reflex defensive movement formed to lighting the cage by a bright electric light (100 or 200 cp) after more than a hundred pairings with the defensive movement cannot be considered to constitute a genuine conditioned reflex. We know that the very same lighting of the cage evokes a definite response in frogs, i.e., turning the head and the eyes away from the light, a jump, or a slow movement, and sometimes even crossing from the lighted portion into the dark portion (Beburishvili and Chichinadze, 1936). In young frogs, this is observed as a rule (Leutskii, 1929), and probably in adult frogs such an illumination evokes a motor reaction more strongly and more frequently by the same innate pathway than prior to pairing with the electrical stimulation. Thus, it should be noted that for both electrical stimuli and in response to a conditional lighting, the frog does not manifest goal-directed motion toward the passageway from the illuminated portion into the dark portion. The frog passed over it when the passageway was found in its field of vision (Beburishvili and Chichinadze, 1936). This fact best indicates that the frog moves as a result of the light stimulation into the dark section as a result of an innate pathway.

Memory in Summer Frogs. After these frogs had become accustomed to the experimental arrangement, they began to catch live worms, even from the hand of the experimenter, as the worm, held with tweezers, was brought close to the frog's mouth. They also swallowed a strip of meat if it were shaken in front of their eyes.

Experiments on feeding behavior of these frogs were carried out in the summer season in a small terrarium. Along one of its walls, there was a wooden bar, on which the frog learned to sit quietly. Along the opposite wall stood two small screens, behind which was affixed a stick with a point, onto which a worm was placed at the time of an experiment. Along the same wall, between these screens, an electric lamp was hung, to the light of which a conditioned approach to the screen for food was elaborated.

These experiments were carried out in the Physiological Laboratory of Tbilisi State University by my colleague M. Maisuradze (1970).

In one series of experiments, 5 to 10 sec after lighting the lamp, the frog was driven behind one of the screens with a stick, and seeing the worm there, seized it with the tongue and swallowed it. These feedings in association with the light were carried out for 3 to 5 min. At first, the frog did not respond to the conditional light; only after repeated feedings did it begin to respond by quivering and after scores of feedings began itself to go to the feeder. Thus, in one frog, the experiments were carried out over 14 days with 94 feedings, and it was characteristic that not once did the frog go to the food at the beginning of an experimental day, but only after several times of being forcibly directed and fed.

During this time, it was also noted that each day after several feedings associated with the light, the frog itself went directly to the screen with food in the absence of the light signal. This occurred for several minutes after the last feeding, and means that the images of the location of food were retained in the memory of the frog for some minutes.

But the experiments also showed that if the food was inedible, for example, if the strip of meat had been soaked with an unpleasant substance such as oil of cloves, the frog after the very first touching of it with the tongue rejected it and refused altogether to seize a moving strip of meat for several hours. At the same time, another type of moving food, i.e., worms, continued to be swallowed. Only on the second day did the frog begin to eat the strip of meat equally with the worms. From this it follows that the visual image of a once-perceived food object that is unpleasant to the taste is retained in memory for hours. It is evident that in frogs the swallowing of movable objects is an innate reflex. That the frog always seizes certain moving objects but not others from the usual environment with the tongue and swallows them constitutes an individually-acquired act, i.e., it is a manifestation of image memory in trials with moving objects after an appreciable interval of time. In the instance of repeated trials after short intervals, it is conditioned-reflex memory. This must be the case both for food objects that are accepted as well as for ones that are rejected.

In another series of experiments, defensive behavior was studied in frogs that had just completed metamorphosis. The experiments were carried out in a small aquarium, at one end of which there were two sections. In the first of these, electrode plates for stimulation were introduced. The frogs preferred to be in this section, for it was darker and quieter there.

If under these conditions, the frog was stimulated with an electrical current, it swam out of that section and did not return to it again. If during this time the water was bubbled, the frog became frightened and swam into another section. If it were driven into the first section wired with electrodes, with the aid of a stick, it went out of the water and crawled to the wall. When the electrode plates were transferred into the second section, the frog immediately ceased swimming there. In the course of some hours after a single electrical painful stimulation, the frog avoided that section where the electrodes were located. Only on the next day was it possible to see the frog in the water of that section where it had undergone stimulation, despite the presence of the electrodes.

From this it follows that in frogs, the perception of the electrodes is associated with the noxious effect of the water of that section where these electrodes were located. Moreover, this association can result from the sight of the electrodes in the course of several hours after the electrical stimulation. This means that in frogs, emotional memory in the form of fear for a noxious agent is retained for several hours, but does not persist until the next day.

Conditioned-defensive behavior in young frogs in the first days after metamorphosis was also studied in summer months. The experiments were carried out as in the preceding ones, in a small aquarium which was divided by means of a partition into two sections. There was an opening in the partition through which the animal could pass from the one to the other section. One section was small, into which the electrodes were lowered, and here there was also placed a red light bulb. For the experiments, the frog was placed in this section and at intervals of 3 to 5 min, was stimulated electrically for 3 to 5 sec after the bulb was lit. Up to 20 pairings were carried out on a given day.

Turning on the light itself did not evoke movement, but after 6 to 10 pairings of the light with the electrical stimulation, the frog responded by movement at the same spot, and after 16 to 20 pairings, it began to go over into the other section from time to time. Similarly, it went into the second section from time to time on the following day as well. Only after a number of days, e.g., on the eighth day, did the frog begin to respond with a conditioned movement into the other section at the beginning of an experimental day. But after an interruption of five days, the conditioned behavior was absent, and it was necessary to carry out several pairings as a preliminary.

Thus, it is evident that in summer frogs, both image and emotional memory is developed comparatively well, whereas conditioned-reflex memory is developed very poorly.

Memory in Tritons. Experiments were also carried out on tritons in winter and in summer. They manifested image and emotional memory both in summer and in winter, but they lived both in the winter and in the summer in the laboratory at a temperature of 17–20°C. In contradistinction to frogs, tritons took in food in both seasons, seizing and swallowing moving worms and strips of meat. However, image and emotional memory in tritons in both seasons appeared significantly weaker than in summer frogs.

Especially characteristic for these amphibia is the fact that the capability for both conditioned-reflex feeding and for defensive behavior is low. Both feeding and conditioned-defensive behavior is elaborated after several scores of pairings of the conditional signal with the unconditional one, and is retained for a few days (these experiments on tritons were also carried out by M. Maisuradze).

In comparison with bony fish, we must conclude that image and emotional memory in amphibia are developed somewhat better than in fish, but conditioned-reflex activity in amphibia is significantly inferior to that in fish.

The following can be proposed, in relation to the origin of this difference.

Image and emotional activity are dependent on the forebrain, and they evidently develop in frogs to a significantly greater extent than in bony fish. Conditioned-reflex activity in bony fish is regulated in the main by the cerebellum and by the medial parts of the brain. In amphibia, on the other hand, the cerebellum is very poorly developed, and it is evident that it does not play an essential role in the formation of conditioned reflexes. Further, as the histological studies of Herrick (1927) showed, the medial parts of the brain of frogs are developed significantly less than in bony fish. Herrick found that the amphibian has undergone an involution and, as a result of this, the brains of amphibia are less differentiated than in bony fish; the nervous system of the former retains very few specific cellular centers and neural pathways. Each neuron is connected with almost all of the remaining ones, which are favorable to generalized responses. In bony fish, on the other hand, the brain is more differentiated and excitation is conducted by more compact pathways between specially developed neural centers of the midbrain and the diencephalon, in almost the same way as in cerebral hemispheres. Perhaps, then, the paradoxical peculiarity of amphibia in relation to conditioned behavior is explained by the structural peculiarity of the intermediate parts of their brain.

Image Memory in Reptiles. Image memory was also studied in turtles and lizards. The experiments were carried out on marsh turtles and in a terrarium of dimensions 130 $\times$ 80 cm. One of the four quarters of the terrarium was divided off from the remaining part by means of a transparent partition made of plexiglass. The turtles were located in this part between experiments. The other end of the terrarium was divided by opaque partitions into three sections in which the turtles were fed at the time of the experiments.

The turtles were well acclimated to the experimental environment and to the experimenter, which took more than a few days; in time, they became accustomed to receiving food from the hand of the experimenter, in which a piece of meat was put by pincers. Usually, the turtles were located in the terrarium in a part in which there was water, but in the second part, there was no water, the arrangement being that the animal could freely move to soil and back again. There was always a reflecting heater above the terrarium and the temperature in it did not fall below 35–36°C; during an experiment, the temperature was raised to 36–37°C (El'darov and Sikharulidze, 1968).

It is necessary to explain these experimental conditions. If the experiments were begun before acclimatization to this warm environment, then not only was it impossible to observe image-driven behavior, but also the formation of conditioned-reflex behavior.

The experiments were carried out in the spring and summer months on European (*Emys orbicularis*) and Caspian (*Clemmus caspica*) turtles. It was noted that Caspian turtles are more easily frightened and became accustomed more slowly to the experimental conditions than the European turtles, but no other difference in their behavior was evident.

The following experiments were carried out on marsh turtles in order to study image memory of an isolated visual perception of the feeding object: Food was shown through a partition to the turtle located in one of the sections (No.4) of the terrarium, and then the food was placed in one of the other parts, No. 1, 2, or 3. After varying intervals of time, the turtle was released from the section where it was located (No. 4). It was found that for 2 to 2½ min following the showing of the food, turtles correctly went to the location of food and found it. For longer intervals between the showing of the food and the turtle's release from section No. 4, they made errors in choosing the direction of the location of food.

The role of olfaction in the experiments mentioned was excluded: First, the food was shown to the turtles through a transparent partition, so that the odor of the food could not pass through to them, and secondly, special experiments convinced us that even at a distance of 8 to 10 cm, the turtles could not find the food by olfaction.

In the following series of experiments, we studied image memory in turtles after complex perception of the food, in which vestibular stimulation, olfaction, and taste participated. The turtles were put into one of the feeding sections and given food; part of the food remained in the same place. Then the animals were returned to their own quarters. After specific intervals of time, they were released and their behavior was observed. The turtles correctly went to the place of food for 3 to 3½ min, but they could not find the food after longer intervals of time.

In another series of experiments, we placed partitions on the path to the food. Turtles did not immediately go around the obstacle; they went up to the partition, stopped and looked at it. But afterwards they immediately began to go around it. In this way, the turtles showed that they retained in memory the location of the food and by reproduction of the image of it, they could exactly project the image into the environment.

Conditioned-Reflex Memory in Marsh Turtles. In the same marsh turtles, initially El'darov (1967) and then El'darov and Sikharulidze (1968) studied conditioned-feeding behavior. Of course, as a preliminary, these turtles were also acclimated to the situation of the experiment. During an experiment they were maintained at a temperature of 36–37°C.

El'darov (1967) established conditioned reflexes of a rather complex character. At first the animals were taught to pull on a specially constructed mouthpiece and to take food from a feeder, pressing on its door with the snout. Both feeder and mouthpiece were located above the water. For consolidation of these movements, 100 to 150 pairings were necessary. Following this, the animals elaborated a conditioned response of securing food from the feeder in response to illumination with a green light bulb inserted in the mouthpiece, using the principle of random coincidence: At the moment the animal pulled, the lamp was turned on and then the trap door was opened. After 3 to 25 pairings in response to the green light, the turtle took the mouthpiece and immediately pushed on the trap door and received food. The reflex was consolidated after 11 to 41 pairings.

El'darov also succeeded in establishing differentiation to a red light. At first, the turtle also took the mouthpiece in response to the red light, but did not receive food. After 3 to 5 trials, it ceased taking the mouthpiece and pressing the trap door of the feeder.

Both positive conditioned reflex and differentiated behavior were found to be quite stable, and the animals responded correctly for a period of 1 to $1\frac{1}{2}$ months.

El'darov and Sikharulidze also established a conditioned feeding response to the illumination by a green electric light by means of pairing it with the delivery of food from the feeder. After 25 to 35 feedings, it was sufficient for the experimenter to turn on the lamp in order for the turtle to begin to secure food. This conditioned reflex was consolidated after 50 to 60 pairings. The turning of the green light was continued for 10 to 15 sec, and on each experimental day there were 10 to 15 pairings. The reflex was consolidated to such a degree that it could be evoked in some turtles 1 to $1\frac{1}{2}$ months after the last trial with feeding. Differentiation to the red light was achieved rather rapidly, after 10 to 15 presentations.

Thus, *in marsh turtles image feeding behavior is manifest for 3 to $3\frac{1}{2}$ min following perception of the food object. Conditioned-reflex feeding behavior to light is elaborated after repeated pairings and is retained for longer than a month.* This means that image memory to the food object is of a short-term character and the image of it can be reproduced for 3 to $3\frac{1}{2}$ min, but conditioned-reflex memory is retained for more than a month.

Emotional Memory in Turtles. Emotional memory to painful stimulation, with the outward manifestation of fear, was studied in land turtles (Sikharulidze, 1966). The experiments were set up according to the same method as for frogs.

The experimental turtle was placed in a compartment containing a wired floor, where it could be subjected to electrical stimulation, and was left there for a number of days, usually staying in the same corner, as though it had become accustomed to this location. Upon electrical stimulation, the animal began to move about vigorously, breathed intermittently, and moved quickly to another section. This activity and intermittent respiration lasted for 2 to 3 min. If at this time it was transferred back to the conducting section, it immediately moved quickly to another section, despite the absence of stimulation. Such behavior of the turtle was observed even after it had become quiet, if it was transferred back to the wired portion not later than 4 to 5 min following stimulation. Only later could it be placed again in this section and remain quiet, as prior to stimulation. This was the case for all ground turtles observed.

On the other hand, if the turtle was stimulated a few times in sequence, then it was noted that even if it was placed in the wired section on the next day, it quickly left the latter and moved into another section. This means that the sight of the conducting section or touching the conductor reproduced the emotion of fear, thus compelling escape into the other section.

In the same way, a conditioned-defensive reflex to the light of the electric lamp was established in the land turtle. After 23 to 27 pairings of the illumination with the painful electrical stimulation, the turtle quickly moved into the other section in response to the light alone. This conditioned reflex appeared even two or three weeks after the last electrical stimulation. It was possible to differentiate white light from red after 10 to 15 trials of the red light without pairing with the electrical stimulation, but the differentiation was unstable and was not retained on the following day (Sikharulidze, 1966).

Thus, *the land turtle retains in memory a single occasion of the perception of a location of painful stimulation for 4 to 5 min. But after repeated stimulation in a single experimental day, the turtle, when it was placed on the next day in the wired section, immediately went to the other section. This means that the emotional memory of fear for the painful stimulation in the land turtle is significantly stronger than in fish. Conditioned-reflex memory to painful stimulation in turtles is also developed to a significantly greater extent than in fish.*

Memory Following Removal of the Forebrain in Turtles. Conditioned-reflex activity is retained after removal of the forebrain, although differentiation of the red from the yellow light disappears, i.e., when the conditioned feeding behavior has been established to the red light, the animal is unable to differentiate it from the yellow light. Image memory after complex perception of a new place of food is strongly disturbed: Operated turtles correctly go to the place of food for only 20 to 30 sec, whereas prior to operation, they would go for 3 to $3\frac{1}{2}$ min. In exactly the same way, image memory for a conditioned stimulus was disturbed: They could go correctly to the location of food for a period of 20 sec after the latter had been signaled, but not for an interval of 4 to 5 min, as had been the case prior to operation. This was apparent even 1 to $1\frac{1}{2}$ months after operation.

In the same operated turtles, Sikharulidze observed that emotional memory for painful electrical stimulation was also strongly impaired. They avoided the place of stimulation only for an interval of 20 to 25 sec, rather than for 3 to 4 min, as had been the case prior to operation.

Thus, in turtles, image and emotional memory are a function of the forebrain, whereas conditioned-reflex memory is a function of the other parts of the brain.

Image Memory in Lizards. Image behavior in lizards was studied in a specially constructed terrarium, the bottom of which was covered with a thick layer of sand with stones and shells, in which the lizard could hide. The sand was moistened daily. Part of the terrarium from one wall was enclosed by an opaque partition. The animals remained there all of the time in the periods between experiments. Another side of the terrarium was separated by a transparent partition; the animals were placed here during an experiment. Raising the partitions released them into the large middle portion of the terrarium.

As a preliminary, the lizards were acclimated to the experimental conditions. Initially, they were frightened by the novelty of the experimental situation, and also of the experimenter. When, by means of a metallic ruler, the lizard was forced near the food, the animal attempted to defend itself, and did not take food. But when it itself caught sight of the food, it did eat. Subsequently, the lizards became so accustomed to the conditions of the experiment that they could be brought to the food and returned again behind the partition with the aid of the ruler.

The experiments with image behavior for study of memory in lizards were carried out by Sikharulidze (1966). In one series of experiments, lizards were shown a feeder with food through a transparent partition, and then were placed behind some rock or shell, at a distance of 30–70 cm, so that they could not see the food. Then, after various intervals of time, the partition was raised and the animal released. It was found that in such cases the lizards go directly to the place of food even after an interval of several minutes. In winter and generally on cold days, the maximum of remembering of once perceived food was $1\frac{1}{2}$ to $2\frac{1}{2}$ min, while in the summer months (June, July, and August), when the animals got more active, the maximum delay was $2\frac{1}{2}$–3 min. If the intervals were longer, they also went out, but ran about the terrarium and ate the food only if it happened to see it.

It was noteworthy that if the lizard was released soon after being shown the food, it attempted to run directly to the place of food. But if it was released later, it moved about slowly and, from time to time, became fixed in one posture for some seconds. This condition of motionlessness had the character of an orienting response. Presumably, the psychoneural process of the image of the food was sufficiently strong soon after the animal was shown the food so that rapid movement toward the place of food was evoked, thus making impossible the perception of the environment in detail, and hence, the corresponding orienting response in the form of motionlessness did not occur.

If the path to the place of food is specifically obstructed, lizards quickly try to climb over the obstacle. If this is found to be impossible, after several failures, they begin to go around the obstacle (Sikharulidze, 1966).

In another series of experiments, the lizard was directed by means of the ruler to food located behind some particular shell and allowed to eat it entirely, or only partially. Then the animal was again directed behind the partition, with the aid of the ruler. After raising the partition, it acted as though it had been shown the food at a distance. During the winter months, the lizards went directly to the food after 2 to $2\frac{1}{2}$ min, and during the summer months after 3 to $3\frac{1}{2}$ min. For longer intervals, the image of the place of food was not produced; it did not carry over to the next day.

Thus, *in lizards, as in turtles, a single visual perception of food establishes an image of the latter which is projected into a specific location; this image is retained for 2 to $2\frac{1}{2}$ min. Lizards can go directly to a place of food in accordance with this image, without interruption and without stops of an orienting character. Moreover, they surmount obstacles standing in the way by crawling over them or going around them, carrying out these motions in accordance with the projection of the image of the location of food.*

Emotional Memory in Lizards. N. Sikharulidze and A. Kadagishvili (1969) have also studied emotional memory in lizards. During the action of conditioned signals while feeding, they stimulated lizards with electrical current through a metallic plate on which the animal was placed during the act of feeding. In response to electrical stimulation, the lizards jumped off the feeding plate. Again the conditioned signal was delivered, but within 4 to 5 min after stimulation they did not go to the location of food.

If the lizards were released from their usual location without the conditioned signal, but after an interval no longer than 3 to $3\frac{1}{2}$ min following stimulation, they would not approach the location of food, but they would do so after a longer interval.

Thus, *emotional fear directed to the location of a damaging agent is maintained for 4 to 5 min after stimulation.*

Memory in Lizards Following Ablation of the Telencephalon. In one series of experiments, N. Sikharulidze and A. Kadagishvili (1969) removed the entire telencephalon, while in the other only the cerebellum was removed.

Following the removal of the telencephalon, the remembering of the location of food objects was disturbed for the isolated visual perception of the food objects, as well as for their complex perception with all the sense organs. While intact lizards went correctly to the location of the perceived food objects after an interval of 3 to $3\frac{1}{2}$ min, the operated ones were able to go correctly after perception to the location of food only within 10 to 15 sec. After longer intervals, they either would not leave their compartment, or if they did, took a wrong direction toward the food. The same holds for several months after the operation; there were no recoveries of memory.

Conditioned reflexes were not disturbed after ablation of the telencephalon. However, there was impairment in the differentiation of red and yellow lights. Moreover, it should be noted that following ablation of the entire telencephalon, visual and auditory conditioned reflexes, regardless of their manifold reinforcements, were maintained only within an interval of 3 to 5 days, while in intact lizards these reflexes were observed during a 3 to 4 week interval.

Furthermore, following ablation of the entire telencephalon, re-establishment of conditioned reflexes was more difficult than in intact lizards. In the operated animals, almost twice as many reinforcements of the conditional signal with the unconditional one were required.

Delayed reactions to conditioned stimuli seemed to have disappeared. The operated lizards could go correctly to the signaled chamber only during an interval of 10 to 15 sec.

Thus, *following ablation of the telencephalon in lizards, image memory disappears altogether and conditioned-reflex memory is very much impaired.*

In the operated lizards, we have also tested memory of the place where they had been electrically stimulated. Our experiments have shown that the operated lizards, in contrast to the intact ones, could be coaxed with a stick to go to the place where some 20 to 30 sec before they had received electrical stimulation; they did not react at all to it and kept sitting there quietly.

But in the case of a stronger stimulation, the lizards rapidly jumped off the metallic plate and when directed back to the plate after withdrawal of stimulation they momentarily avoided it. This lasted for 10 to 15 sec after electrical stimulation; during this time they did not approach the location of food. However, after an interval of 10 to 15 sec, they went to the location of food where they had received electrical stimulation.

Thus, *in lizards without the telencephalon image memory, as well as emotional memory of fear, have entirely disappeared. As to the conditioned-reflex memory, it is maintained, though strongly impaired.*

Memory after Removal of the Cerebellum. In the first 2 to 3 days after operation, the lizards became less mobile. The impression was that muscle tone was entirely lacking; they were not able to rise on their paws and walk.

Recovery of the motor function proceeded very slowly. Even four months after surgery a complete compensation for the motor disturbances was not yet observed.

It was demonstrated that after either an isolated visual or multisensory complex perception (involving several sensory modalities) of food objects, the lizards devoid of the cerebellum remembered the perceived object as well as the intact ones did. More precisely, the maximum delay for the isolated visual perception approached $2\frac{1}{2}$ to 3 min and for a complex perception 3 to 4 min; no difference was observed between the intact and operated lizards in their memory of the place of noxious stimuli, i.e., feeling fear of the damaging agent.

After removal of the cerebellum, the conditioned reflexes to light and sound existing before surgery were strongly disturbed. In response to the conditioned signals, they went on a zig-zag course toward the feeder, but in the majority of cases they did not reach the food. New conditioned reflexes could be established, but with much difficulty; twice as many reinforcements were required than in intact animals.

However, after the conditioned reflexes were restored, the lizards had all the characteristics of intact organisms. For example, delayed reactions to conditioned stimuli in the operated lizards proceeded normally, i.e., the maximum delay with a conditioned stimulus approached $2\frac{1}{2}$ to $3\frac{1}{2}$ min.

From the foregoing it follows that *in lizards, as in all the reptiles, the cerebellum is as well developed as in bony fish; their cerebellum, however, plays no essential role in the conditioned-reflex activity.*

Conditioned-Reflex Memory in Lizards. Conditioned feeding-movement reflexes in lizards are formed to sound and to light after 15 to 20 feedings in the course of 2 to 3 days. After some reinforcement (50 to 60 pairings), this reflex is quite evident several days later, at the beginning of an experimental day.

When this individual behavior had become well consolidated, experiments were carried out with delayed responses to conditional signals. The signals were presented for 5 sec, and the partition was raised after different intervals of time. It was established that the lizard could go directly to the place of food that had been signaled, during cold months no later than after 1 to $1\frac{1}{2}$ min, but during the summer months no later than after 3 to $3\frac{1}{2}$ min. If the partition was raised soon after the signal, within this interval of time, the lizard went directly to the food place; if the delay were longer, the animal stopped on the way and remained motionless for some time. This means that *in lizards, the image of the location of food reproduced by a conditional signal is retained for the same amount of time as after a single showing or eating of the food. Evidently, the motor activity corresponding to the image of the place of food reproduced following the conditional signal is the same as that following perception of it directly, and that both the one and the other memory disappear over the same interval of time.*

Image Memory in Birds. In birds (chickens and pigeons), image memory for feeding behavior after a single instance of being shown food (which was then placed behind a screen) was retained for 2 to 3 min. But if the chicken is carried to food in a new place and allowed to peck a part of the grain, and then taken into the cage, image memory is retained for 5 to 10 min. This is short-term memory, but this feeding motor response still appears after 1 to 5 days, i.e., as long-term memory. *This means that in birds, short-term memory for feeding objects appears for the first time in the phylogenetic series* (Chichinadze, 1969).

We studied emotional memory in pigeons by means other than electrical stimulation. For study of imitation in pigeons, we formed feeding behavior to a conditional sound toward one of the feeders in one group, while another group was trained to remain quiet in a particular location in the given experimental arrangement. Afterwards, a pigeon of the second group was placed with one of the pigeons in the first group, in which conditioned feeding behavior had been established. When the first pigeon ran to the feeder in response to the auditory signal, the second pigeon followed after some seconds, after seeing the pecking movements of the first. We kept the feeder closed until the pigeon went up to it. The pigeons then fought and the experimenter had to separate them. Subsequently, the second pigeon had a negative effect on the first one; in the second experiment, in response to the signal, the first pigeon approached the feeder only after the latter had been opened. Then the second pigeon also approached, and again they fought. After this, the first pigeon ceased to go upon the conditional signal to the feeder if the second pigeon was present, but if the latter was taken away, the first went to the feeder as usual. This work had to be interrupted for a month, but even after this interruption, if these two pigeons resided together, the first did not go to the feeder; only after the second was removed would the first go on signal. The negative influence of the second pigeon was long lasting, so that the unfavorable emotional conditions were reproduced upon sight of the second pigeon, and this suppressed the feeding behavior of the first (Akhmeteli, 1941).

Thus, *in the pigeon, emotional memory for an aggressive relationship to another pigeon in a given circumstance is retained for more than a month. Consequently, emotional memory in birds is more strongly developed than in reptiles.*

In birds, conditioned-reflex memory is also developed to a significantly greater extent than in reptiles. From the above mentioned experiment, it was already evident that after an interval of a month, the first pigeon would go to the feeder upon signal if an aggressive pigeon was not present. We did not attempt to establish the maximum time of retention of the learned feeding behavior, but it can be stated that it must be appreciably longer than one month.

Memory after Removal of a Part of the Forebrain in Birds. The neocortex is less developed in birds than in mammals. If the dorsal and lateral surface of the neocortex is removed in chickens, without damaging the medial portion, the animal can scarcely be distinguished in its behavior from normal. The capability of orientation in space is retained, as is the capability of finding food independently. If food is shown behind a screen, then the bird will go by itself to the screen, but it is not able to go around it immediately and obtain the food. In chickens, conditioned reflexes to sound and light are retained and can be formed anew after operation, but they do not become automatic as readily as in normal chickens (Kadzhaya, 1962).

Image Memory in Decorticate Chickens. After removal of the entire cortical lamella (i.e., the dorsal medial surface of the forebrain), the capability of independent intake of food is retained in chickens; from their behavior outside of the experimental room, they could not be distinguished from normal chickens; but within the experimental room, they became excitable, appeared restless, attempted to get out of the cage, and carried out searching and pecking movements uninterruptedly. Apparently, the sight of the experimental environment and the experimenter reproduced the image of the operative procedure, attended by fear. In decorticate chickens, image memory was lacking to a significant degree. The maximum interval of delayed responses to the location of food was significantly diminished. The maximum delay for visual perception (i.e., a basin with grain shown close to the front of the cage and slowly carried away behind the screen) did not exceed 15 sec. In this connection, it should be noted that if the basin was placed somewhat further from the cage, the chickens began searching and pecking movements, and could not reach the food screen directly. In relation to the maximum delay for "multisensory complex perception" of the location of food (carrying the decorticate chickens to the basin behind the screen, and allowing them to peck and then returning them to the cage again), such a chicken could go directly to the screen for up to one minute afterwards.

In more complex situations, e.g., if there are three screens standing in the experimental room, decorticate chickens are completely disoriented. After being transported to one of the screens, pecking, and then being returned again to the cage, they go incorrectly even if they are then released from the cage with no delay whatsoever. On each new experimental day, decorticate chickens selected one or another screen and went to it independently of whether they had eaten food there the last time. However, conditioned-reflex activity is not disturbed in such decorticate chickens; existing conditioned reflexes are retained, and new ones can be formed (Kadzhaya, 1962).

Behavior is appreciably disturbed following removal of the hyperstriatum together with the neocortex. Orientation in space is lacking after operation, as are conditioned feeding-movement reflexes to light and to sound, although the animals respond to these stimuli with an orienting response. Feeding-movement reflexes can be formed anew, but require considerably more feedings than in normal chickens, and, even so, the cage must be moved to a distance of less than 2 m from the feeder. The animals themselves do not go directly to the feeder without the signal. Image memory is completely lacking in the animals, as is the ability to obtain food without assistance, but the latter is subsequently gradually restored, after 1 to 5 months following operation.

Therefore, *in birds, the cortical lamella together with the hyperstriatum subserves the function of the neocortex of mammals.*

When both hemispheres of the forebrain are removed entirely, the capability of conditioned-reflex activity also disappears (Kadzhaya, 1962).

These findings mean that image memory is a function of the neocortex and hyperstriatum, and that conditioned-reflex memory is dependent, not only on this part of the forebrain, but also on its remaining parts.

Emotional Memory in Chickens. Chickens became accustomed to the experimental environment, to standing in the cage at a specific place, to walking at the sound of a bell to screen No. 1, to a tone to screen No. 2, and to returning by the same path to the starting point after feeding. The two screens stood at a distance of 3 m from the cage. Behind the first screen there was a basin with a piece of felt glued to the bottom on a metallic plate. Water was poured into the basin and grain was added to the water. If the metallic plate and the basin were connected with a source of current, then with the very first pecking, the chicken was subjected to electrical stimulation.

After clearly automatized feeding behavior was established as in a normal chicken to the sound of a bell, in relation to a basin behind screen No. 1, and to a tone, in relation to a basin behind screen No. 2, the chicken was subjected to electrical stimulation (120 V) at screen No. 1, i.e., for feeding behavior following the ringing of the bell; it jumped away from the basin frightened and guardedly extended the neck and glanced around. We then returned the chicken to the cage. For 10 min following the electrical stimulation, the chicken would not go out of the cage when the bell sounded. After 11 min following the electrical stimulation, the chicken went out of the cage when the tone sounded and went correctly in the direction of screen No. 2, but then flew to the window, thus not reaching the basin. We then returned the chicken to the cage. But now, after 12 min following electrical stimulation, the chicken went correctly and confidently to the basin behind screen No. 2 in response to the tone and began to peck grain. We then returned the chicken to the cage. After 13 min following electrical stimulation, the chicken was brought out of the cage by hand and placed at the basin behind the first screen, but it did not peck. It was then returned to the cage. After 15 min and 30 min following electrical stimulation, the chicken remained in the cage in response to the bell. After 5 hr following electrical stimulation, the chicken did go out of the cage in response to the bell, but very cautiously going first to screen No. 2, and not seeing food there, finally went to screen No. 1 and began to peck in a very frightened manner.

After electrical stimulation on the second day, the chicken went out of the cage when the bell sounded and went correctly to screen No. 1, and very cautiously and fearfully went up to the basin and made only a single pecking motion, turned, and slowly returned to the cage completely spontaneously. When the tone was sounded on the second day after electrical stimulation, the chicken went readily without any fear to screen No. 2 and began to peck. On the third day after electrical stimulation, the chicken went out of the cage when the bell sounded, went in the direction of screen No. 2 and not seeing food there, went very cautiously in the direction of screen No. 1 and began to eat. This condition lasted for two weeks. Only in the third week was normal automatized feeding behavior in response to the bell restored (Kadzhaya, 1970).

Thus, *both image and emotional memory in a representative bird, i.e., the chicken, are developed somewhat better than in reptiles.*

Emotional memory was also studied in the chicken after removal of the neocortex. If such a chicken is subjected to painful stimulation by means of an electrical current while carrying out automatized feeding behavior in response to a bell, then in contradistinction to a normal chicken, it does not immediately run away from the basin. When we sounded the bell, the chicken went to the basin behind screen No. 1 and with the very first pecking perceived the electrical current (120 V), whereupon it immediately ceased pecking the grain. After a few seconds, it again began pecking, again perceived the current, again stopped, and only after perceiving the current for the third time, when it resumed eating once again, did it go away from the basin, relatively quietly. We then took the chicken back to the cage. Five minutes after electrical stimulation, we sounded the bell. The decorticate chicken, in contradistinction to the normal, went out of the cage to screen No. 2; not finding food there, it began to walk all about the room, but did not go up to screen No. 1. Eight minutes after electrical stimulation, we sounded the tone. The chicken went out of the cage, went quickly to the basin behind screen No. 2, and began to peck. Fifteen minutes after electrical stimulation we sounded the bell. The chicken was released from the cage, and brought up to the bowl behind screen No. 2. In contrast to the normal chicken, it began pecking. Thirty minutes after electrical stimulation, we sounded the bell. The chicken went out of the cage and up to screen No. 2; not finding food there, it began to go about the room, and went spontaneously up to the basin behind screen No. 1 and began to peck. This situation continued for five days. On the sixth day, normal feeding behavior to the bell, i.e., towards screen No. 1, was restored (Kadzhaya, 1969).

Thus, *decorticate birds possess emotional memory to a smaller degree than normal. This undoubtedly depends on the fact that image memory of the neocortex no longer participates in the reproduction of the location of the stimulating agent, i.e., the operative procedure.*

Memory in Mammals. Among mammals, memory was investigated in detail in rabbits, cats, and dogs. Memory in the latter has already been considered in detail earlier. Analogous experiments were carried out with rabbits and cats. A basic condition for the appearance of memory in full measure is the acclimatization of the animals to the conditions of the experiment. This was appreciably more difficult in the case of rabbits. It was necessary to spend some weeks with them in order to accustom them to remaining quietly in the cage, to moving freely about the experimental room, and to reacting quietly to the approach of the experimenter and his manipulations.

In rabbits, following complete accommodation to the conditions of the experiment, memory for visual perception of a food object and its location was appreciably better than in chickens. But all rabbits were extremely active and fearful. With time, they became accustomed to the conditions of the experiment and gradually became quieter. Correspondingly, short-term memory to visual perception of the place of food was initially very short. In the first days of the work, when they were still in the cage, they were very restless, moving all the time and shaking the cage, and after being shown the food, they went to the place of food behind a screen for not more than 20 to 25 sec later. After a month of work, they seemed appreciably quieter, and went directly to the location of food for 2 to 3 min, and only after 5 months or more was the maximum interval 7 to 10 min (Gelashvili, 1968), or as much as 15 to 20 min (Chichinadze, 1967) established.

In the first few days following "multisensory complex perception" of food in a new place in which both taste and olfaction participated, rabbits went there after 50 to 60 sec. But after one month, they went 3 to 4 min after feeding, and after 3 months of work, a 15 to 16 min interval could ensue, and still later they went even after 20 min (Gelashvili, 1968).

But if, after feeding in a new place, the rabbit was brought from the cage into the vivarium and returned again after an hour or even on the next day, it would go to the location of food immediately or after a few searching movements around the cage. The same behavior could be observed 6 to 8 days after feeding (Chichinadze, 1967). Evidently, if the external environment does not change after feeding, then the absence of novelty in the environment leads to a pronounced limitation of the orienting response; in particular, it leads to elimination of that orienting response which could serve for reproduction of the image of the location of food. This occurs, as pointed out previously, as a result of adaptation to the unchanging environment.

Conditioned reflex memory in rabbits to feeding behavior toward a specific feeder, in response to a particular signal, can appear 10 days later, although in somewhat weaker form, such that the animal goes with an appreciable delay (e.g., 10 sec). Two months later, the feeding reflex appears only as chewing and swallowing movements; the rabbits do not go toward the feeder (Bregadze, 1929).

In cats accustomed to the experimental environment, short-term memory to visual perception of the location of food is limited to 15 to 20 min. But in response to auditory perception of the place of food, produced by striking the basin, a delayed response can ensue after 3 to 6 min. This interval, on the order of minutes, however, is limited by the absence of novelty in the surrounding environment and the extinction of the orienting response. It is sufficient to bring a cat for 1 to 2 hr into the vivarium and then to bring it back, whereupon it will go directly to the place of food.

Long-term memory to complex perception of food was also studied in cats. It was established that, *following exhibition of food with olfaction or feeding of it in an absolutely new environment, the exact localization of the place of food was remembered for a number of days or even for a month* (Chichinadze, 1967). In this connection, cats differ little from dogs.

Emotional memory in cats was studied by painful stimulation presented during eating. The cat jumped away from the feeder upon stimulation, and ceased approaching it; if the stimulation was weak, this avoidance response was retained for several days. If the stimulation was stronger, the avoidance of a particular feeder was retained for weeks, as in the dog. Thus, *emotional memory to unpleasant stimulation which is related to self-defense is so strong that not only individually-acquired, but also innate feeding-movement responses are inhibited.*

Conditioned-reflex memory in cats is the same as in dogs, which was described in detail in the preceding chapters. Conditioned feeding or defensive reflexes, as well as learned instrumental movements in these animals are elaborated significantly more rapidly and retained for a significantly longer time than in all of the preceding types of animals.

The role of the forebrain and the cerebral cortex in relation to memory in cats and dogs has also been considered in detail in the preceding chapters. It was shown that image memory is more or less significantly impaired following bilateral removal of different regions of the cortex, especially following removal of the proreal gyri and also the temporal lobes, and was totally lacking after removal of the entire neocortex. In the latter case, long-term emotional memory in the form of the response of fear was also lacking. Conditioned-reflex memory, as it appears in normal animals, was also lacking. However, it was possible to establish anew very unstable and simple feeding-conditioned reflexes.

Image Memory in Lower Simians. Recently, we began to study memory in lower simians (Hamadryad baboons) by exactly the same method of free movement as was used for dogs. For the corresponding experimental setup, it was necessary to accustom the animals to the conditions of the experiment, i.e., to live more or less quietly in the cage, to be led freely by the collar from one place to another, and also to move independently about the room. Of particular importance was the necessity of stopping the animals from jumping at objects located in the room. The latter was very difficult to do, but after 2 or 3 months of work, more or less, the monkeys became accustomed to all of the conditions necessary for study of memory in the large experimental room by the method of free movement.

On such acclimatized monkeys, it was already observed in the first trials that short-term memory to a single perception of the location of food was measured in tens of minutes. In subsequent experiments, it was shown that if a piece of apple or candy was shown in a basin, and then the latter was placed behind one of the screens (of which there were six, at a distance of 2 to 5 m), then the monkey went directly to the correct screen as soon as the cage was opened 10, 20, or 30 min later and sometimes even after 60 min. Moreover, if the monkey was led to a new place, shown or given food, and then returned to the vivarium, and was brought back to the experimental room the next day or even after a week, it went directly behind the screen. But if a piece of food was given in some new room, then the monkey might go directly to the location of food after a month and a half, when the animal was brought to the door of this room.

If, after food was shown from behind a new screen, the cage was covered, so that the monkey could not see the screen nor the general experimental environment, then, following release, it went up to this screen, irrespective of its behavior prior to release. The animal might be very restless, shaking the cage, attempting to open the door, crying out continuously, but after opening the door, it went correctly to the screen and ate. It was possible also to take the monkey out of the cage, lead it by the collar about the room, and give it some food during this time, and then shut it up again in the cage. If the cage was then opened, it went to the same screen where it had last eaten food (Beritashvili et al., 1969).

In brief, we were convinced from the very first experiments with delayed responses that *baboons show both short-term and long-term memory to visual or "multisensory complex perception" of the location of food somewhat better than cats and dogs under exactly the same experimental conditions.*

We also studied image memory in baboons following removal of the prefrontal region of the granular area of both hemispheres, which is homologous with the proreal gyrus of lower vertebrates. As would be expected, an appreciable worsening of image memory ensued after removal of the granular area, as had already been observed by other authors. But our method of free movement enabled us to study this defect in detail. In the first weeks following removal, memory to visual perception of the location of food was impaired in the baboon to such a degree that, after being shown food or after being led to the place of food and eating part of it, the animals could not go directly to food even 1 to 3 min later.

Memory then very gradually improved, although even 5 to 7 months later, the animals went to a new location of food for only up to 3 min after being shown it, and 5 to 10 min after eating part of the food (Beritashvili, et al., 1969).

From this it follows that *in lower simians, the prefrontal granular zone must be an important neural substratum for image memory.*

Thus, the phylogenetic development of image memory to the location of food occurs very gradually from fish to monkeys. In lower stages of the development (fish, reptiles), only short-term memory appears; in birds (chickens), short-term memory is more developed. In the latter, long-term memory also appears, although in a very limited form, i.e., up to five days. Among lower mammals (rabbits), both short-term and long-term memory are significantly better than in birds; among higher mammals, such as cats and dogs, both short-term memory (the duration of which usually is of the order of some tens of minutes) and long-term memory (of the order of weeks and months) are significantly longer. In baboons, both short-term and long-term memory are still better manifest than in cats and dogs.

In all of these animals, image memory is a function of the forebrain, and with the development of the neocortex, it becomes basically a function of this cortex.

Emotional memory in the form of fear following a single external noxious agent also develops very gradually from fish to monkeys and is a function of the forebrain. But once the neocortex appears, short-term memory of the emotion of fear is carried out entirely in the old cortex, whereas long-term memory to the emotion of fear is carried out by the neocortex, for it depends on the reproduction of the image of the noxious agent.

Conditioned-reflex memory is a function of the entire brain, but with phylogenetic development, it moves from lower parts such as the cerebellum and the midbrain, generally, to the forebrain, and then to the cerebral cortex.

POSTEMBRYONIC DEVELOPMENT OF MEMORY

Postembryonic development of memory was studied in puppies and kittens; experiments with image memory were carried out on puppies, and experiments with emotional and conditioned-reflex memory were carried out on puppies and kittens.

Image Memory in Puppies. Puppies are devoid of image memory, both in the period 12 to 16 days before eye opening, and in the ensuing period to the age of 30 to 32 days, when they are already walking on erect legs.

At the age of 30 days, puppies were weaned and feeding on milk and small pieces of meat began. For these experiments, the puppies were brought into the experimental room and seated in the closed cage. For several days, they behaved restlessly: they continuously moved about the cage, whined, thrusting out the nose or paw, but then gradually settled down. In this period, the puppies in the cage did not react with an orienting response to a basin of food which was moved just in front of their nose. If the basin was placed on the floor after being shown, then the animals moved randomly around the cage after release from the cage, but did not go directly to the basin as long as the latter was not nearby in the field of vision. Thus, at the age of 30 to 32 days, puppies are devoid of the ability to carry out delayed responses after visual perception of the location of food (Aivazashvili and Partskhaladze, 1968).

The first signs of memory appeared at the age of 35 to 40 days. A puppy was let out of the cage to a new location of food at a distance of $1\frac{1}{2}$ to 2 m, i.e., to one of the screens situated at this distance behind which part of the food was given. Then the animal was brought back to the cage. Upon release from the cage after 15 to 20 sec, it ran directly toward the food location, but held back from the screen and did not go around it. The experimenter had to lead the puppy several times up to the basin behind the screen in order that, subsequently, the animal would itself go around the obstacle standing in the way of the food. This means that goal-directed avoidance of the obstacle cannot occur as a result of an innate reflex pathway, but rather is elaborated as a conditioned reflex, i.e., it is a natural conditioned reflex. On the other hand, in order for the puppy to go around the screen, having seen it, an image of the location of food was necessary, in addition, since in each specific case the animal did not go around any screen, but around the one behind which food had been placed beforehand in view of the animal.

At the age of 42 to 45 days, an orienting response is finally formed in response to showing food at a distance; puppies turn to the side in which the basin is shown, lick their chops, whine, and retain an orienting stance in the direction of the screen until the basin with the food is placed behind the screen. After 10 to 15 sec, when the cage is opened, the animals go to this location. But if an animal is taken behind the screen and fed there, i.e., after complex perception of the location of food, the delay period is increased to 45 to 50 sec, and in one puppy, even to 1 to 2 min.

At ages of 47 to 50 days, typical delayed responses to visual perception of the place of food occurred for intervals of 20 to 30 sec. With still older puppies, the delay period rapidly increased and by 3 to 4 months, the duration of short-term memory for visual perception was as much as 6 to 7 min, and for "multisensory complex perception," 20 to 25 min (Aivazashvili and Partskhaladze, 1968).

Thus, *in the postembryonic development of puppies, the capability of image memory in the form of typical delayed responses both to visual and to "multisensory complex perception" of a location of food appears at the age of 42 to 45 days and reaches almost the full perfection of adult animals at 3 to 4 months.*

Image Memory in Kittens. Very detailed studies were carried out by Bregadze and Akhmeteli (1969) on kittens. They established that memory for complex perception of food and its location could appear at the age of one month in the form of delayed movement to the location of food after 35 sec, if the food was located at a distance of 1 to $1\frac{1}{2}$ m, and after 20 to 30 sec, for a distance of 2 to $2\frac{1}{2}$ m. But in 2- to 3-month-old kittens, the delayed response to "multisensory complex perception" of food at close distances can occur after as long as 2 to 3 min, and at farther distances, after 1 to 2 min. In 6-month-old kittens, with the same perception, the delayed response for shorter distances can occur after 10 to 12 min, and for greater distances, after 8 min.

It is interesting that the long-term memory for "multisensory complex perception" in some kittens is as much as 30 min at the age of $1\frac{1}{2}$ months, and 1 hr at $2\frac{1}{2}$ months; the delayed response can appear after 24 hr at 3 months, and after 2 days at 6 months.

The time of the delayed response in postembryonic development for visual perception of the place of food increases correspondingly: at the age of $2\frac{1}{2}$ months, it is approximately 8 to 9 min for close distances, and for far distances, 1 to 3 min. At 5 to 6 months of age, the maximum delay is 8 to 10 min for close distances and 6 to 8 min for far distances.

Thus, *in the postembryonic development of kittens, the ability of short-term image memory, as judged by delayed responses, appears at the age of one month and is essentially perfected at 5 to 6 months. But long-term memory for this interval does not exceed 2 days.*

Conditioned-Reflex Memory in Puppies. Conditioned reflexes in puppies in the form of avoidance movements around an obstacle were found at an age of 35 to 40 days. But still earlier, at the 30th to 32nd day of age, the animals exhibited the ability of formation of conditioned feeding-movements behavior. After three trials at the same location of food, the animals assumed the correct direction, and after 5 to 6 responses, they went directly to that location (Aivazashvili and Partskhaladze, 1968).

The reflex of feeding to indifferent sound or light stimuli was formed somewhat later, at the age of 38 to 40 days (Obraztsova, 1964).

This means that conditioned-reflex movement to the location of food develops at an earlier age than does movement according to an image, i.e., according to image memory. But even after elaboration of such a conditioned-reflex approach to a particular screen, at the age of 30 to 32 days, if the basin with food is shown and then it is placed to the right or to the left of the cage in a new location, then despite the fact that the puppy turns its head to the side of the basin as though to fixate on the place of food, the animal does not go directly there after release from the cage; instead, it carries out random searching movements. This means that in a 30- to 32-day-old, conditioned-reflex approach to a particular bowl is formed, but the perception of the bowl in the form of a visual image is not retained in memory, and hence, appropriate feeding behavior does not result.

Memory for conditioned-avoidance behavior was also studied in puppies (Topuriya, 1926) and in kittens (Bregadze and Akhmeteli, 1969) at various stages of postembryonic development. These workers established the fact that these reflexes can be formed by means of pairing of an indifferent stimulus with electrical stimulation of the extremity even prior to eye opening. In puppies, this was achieved in response to auditory stimulation by means of pairing with electrical stimulation of the extremity. In kittens, conditioned-avoidance reflexes were formed at 3 to 4 days to tactile stimuli (touching with a brush) and also by means of pairing with electrical stimulation of the paw. The resulting reflex effect was diffuse in character: generalized movement, acceleration of respiration, quivering, and loud whining occurred. However, these reflexes were unstable, and were never retained to the next day. Therefore, it can be presumed that they arose owing to increased excitability in motor centers as a result of electrical stimulation, and to the inclusion of them in the response of irradiation of excitation evoked by the stimulation that had been signaled (in the case of puppies, the auditory stimuli; and for the kittens, the mechanical tactile stimulation of the skin).

In these responses, one could detect the external manifestations of fear, but they were hardly accompanied by the subjective experience of fear with participation of the paleocortex. In all probability, this originated without participation of the cortex, i.e., by means of subcortical structures, since it was observed in adult dogs under the same experimental conditions after removal of the cortex (Popov, 1953).

At later stages of postembryonic development, when 20- to 30-day-old puppies and kittens began to walk about, an avoidance reflex to a conditioned stimulus could be formed after 3 to 4 pairings. The resulting avoidance reflex in the form of generalized restlessness, whining, and an orienting response, was complicated by the lifting of the leg that had been stimulated. In this case, we already had a true conditioned-defensive reflex arising with the participation of the cerebral cortex.

With formation of an avoidance reflex by means of pairing with painful electrical stimulation in animals one month old, the response of fear and its emotional experience and external objective manifestation must have arisen. Topuriya (1926) noted that following a series of pairings, puppies showed a diffuse response of fear even upon being placed on the experimental table where they had undergone stimulation. Moreover, 30-day-old puppies responded in this way even after two pairings. On the third trial of the signaling sound, the puppy responded with opening the eyes, acceleration of breathing, whining, and pricking up the ears, which undoubtedly reflect a reinforced orienting response from fear. This response probably results from the archipaleocortex and is accompanied by the emotion of fear.

Thus, *conditioned-reflex memory and emotional memory both appear in the postembryonic development of memory earlier than does image memory.*

From comparison of postembryonic development of image and conditioned-reflex activity, with their phylogenetic development, it must be presumed that *the earlier postembryonic development of conditioned-reflex activity in comparison with image memory recapitulates their phylogenetic development.*

SUMMARY AND CONCLUSIONS

The present monograph is an attempt to throw light on the phenomena of memory in vertebrates: image, emotional, and conditioned-reflex memory. Image memory was studied by us in relation to a food object and its location, emotional memory in relation to a noxious agent, and conditioned-reflex memory was studied in relation to both a food object and a noxious agent.

We refer to memory as image memory when it is based on the remembering of a once perceived food object and on the reproducing of the image of this object and its location as a result of the action of a part of that object or of the situation in which the perception had taken place. Memory of this kind is short-term if it is retained for a few or many minutes after perception, and if it ceases to be manifest after an interval of several hours, as is the case with the perception of a food object not involving its taste and smell. The presence and duration of short-term memory are ascertained by means of so-called delayed responses, i.e., of appropriate feeding motor behavior performed by the animal some time after its perception of the food object. But duration of short-term memory of the food object is most variable: it is longest for olfactory perception, shorter for visual perception, considerably shorter for auditory, and still shorter for vestibular perception. It also varies quite appreciably for each modality, depending on the experimental conditions.

Memory of a food object is referred to as long-term if the images of the object and of its location are reproduced after the lapse of not only some hours, but also several days subsequent to the perception of the object. This is the case with the perception of a food object involving its smell and taste. The stronger the emotional excitation during food intake, the longer is the location of food retained in memory.

Memory of the presence of food in a particular environment does not wholly disappear over a period of many days even if the animal (dog, cat) had taken food in this environment only once, and was later brought to the place daily in a hungry state but did not find food there. The animal usually recalls the fact of the food being absent in a certain place only for a very short time after having consumed all of the food, and during that time it does not go there.

It was found that no routine events, whatsoever, in the animal's life, such as a drowsy state, sleep, running, an aggressive state, food intake, its being led to the vivarium, etc., affect the retention in its memory of the location of the eaten food. In a hungry state, while performing searching movements for food, it will without fail visit all those places where many days previously it had eaten, provided that it happens to find itself in the appropriate situation.

In mammals, image memory is exclusively a function of the neocortex. Ablation of it results in the disappearance of image memory. However, not all neocortical areas are essential for the retention in memory of images of perceived food objects. Of basic significance for the short-term memory of a visual image of a location of food is the secondary visual area, while for auditory memory the secondary auditory area is responsible. The inferior temporal lobes are related to short-term memory for not only visual and auditory perceptions of the food object, but also for all other modalities.

The proreal gyri in the prefrontal area account for short-term memory of perception of the food object by all receptors. The hippocampus is also found to have a certain relevance to short-term memory.

Bilateral ablation of one or another secondary perceiving area brings about deterioration of memory only for perception of the corresponding modality, and what is more, only for the initial several weeks. Later on, memory gradually recovers, but is not fully restored even after many months. Memory is particularly impaired following removal of the proreal gyri and the inferotemporal lobes. If both the proreal gyrus and the secondary area of a perceiving area, say, auditory, are removed, then memory for auditory perception deteriorates still further.

Following operations with removal of the proreal gyri and the inferotemporal lobes, long-term memory of the location of food is also considerably damaged, but memory of this kind is still evident after perception of the food location during the first several weeks. However, even many months after surgery it is not restored to normal.

Such subcortical structures as the caudate nucleus, reticular formation, lemniscal system, and cerebellum have certain roles to play in the retention in memory of perceived food objects. Following bilateral lesion of these structures, memory deteriorates for a more or less extended period of time as a result of the cessation of one or another group of afferent impulses acting on the neocortex.

Proceeding from some physiological and anatomical evidence, we may assume that all the cortical areas mentioned are bilaterally connected by association pyramidal neurons. Not all the sensory stellate neurons responsible for the subjective reflection of the environment, and certainly none of the projection pyramidal neurons triggering external reactions are involved in these circuits. These neurons are connected with the neural circuits of memory by unilateral pathways from these circuits, i.e., colaterals of the association pyramidal neurons, directly or through internuncial pyramidal neurons, and terminate on certain sensory stellate neurons and on projection pyramidal neurons. Thus, the subjective experience in the form of the image of food and its location, and the external manifestation in the form of orienting response or orientating movement in space occur when these association neurons of the neural circuits are activated.

In this integrated system of neural substrates of memory that participates in image memory, the proreal gyri play a leading role. They are widely connected with premotor and motor cortical areas and with subcortical somatovegetative structures, and all responses are evoked from the proreal gyri: instrumental movements through these motor areas and general behavioral emotional reactions through corticofugal pathways to subcortical formations.

Following bilateral removal of the proreal gyri or the inferotemporal lobes, normal activity of the other areas of memory is temporarily disturbed. This obviously is the result of decreased excitability of the association neurons of other cortical areas, due to the cessation of impulses from the proreal gyri. The more or less considerable subsequent restoration of image memory should be accounted for by a subsequent increase in excitability of the association neurons of the intact areas of memory resulting from their repeated excitation in the individual life of the animal.

Lesion of the secondary area of a perceiving region, for example, of the visual area, disturbs memory only for visual perception but does not bring about any marked impairment of memory for other perceptions, since there is no appreciable resultant effect on all the remaining mass of association neurons of memory.

From the preceding, it follows that the images of perceived objects are not coded in some particular part of the integrated system of neural substrates of memory, for removal of any one of them does not result in the loss of memory. Image memory is lost only after removal of the entire neocortex, i.e., after ablation of all those neocortical pyramidal association neurons which are activated during perception of the object in question.

Short-term memory of the location of food, according to the views of many authors, is based on the reverberation of excitation of the association and internuncial pyramidal neurons of the closed neural circuits of memory. This reverberation may last no longer than some dozens of seconds after the cessation of the impact from the food object. Subsequent to that, short-term memory is apparently based on increased excitability lasting many minutes after reverberation has ceased. This increase of excitability mainly occurs in the synaptic regions under the influence of the mediator released from the presynaptic vesicles that are accumulated during reverberation of excitation.

Over this period of time the neural circuits are readily excitable and the image of the food location is reproduced with corresponding ease when the animal is subsequently acted upon by a part of the same food object or by part of the same situation that had attended the perception of the food object in question. Such a phase of increased excitability may last as much as 20 minutes or even longer in higher vertebrates.

Long-term memory for the location of food is evidently dependent upon molecular and submolecular changes of protein in the activated postsynaptic regions. It is conjectured that with participation of nuclear RNA-intermediary and ribosomal RNA, the synthesis of an active protein is induced, which, acting on the postsynaptic membrane, facilitates transmission of excitation to these regions. When perception of the food object is only visual, the action of this protein may continue for hours. When perception involves taste and smell of the food object and is accompanied by a strong emotional excitation, conditions are apparently extablished in the postsynaptic regions of the above-mentioned neural circuits, such that the effect of the active protein on the postsynaptic membrane is assured for a prolonged time, measured in days or even months.

Emotional memory in the form of fear in relation to a noxious agent and its situation depends on the emergence of association neural circuits in the archi-paleocortex connected with sensory elements of fear, as well as with the subcortical somatovegetative structures responsible for the external manifestations of fear. Reverberation of excitation and subsequent increase of excitability of these neuronal circuits account for short-term memory for the response of fear. But long-term memory for the emotion of fear is presumed to depend on the appearance of active protein in these postsynaptic regions, which produces the image of the noxious agent and its location by activating the association neurons of the neuronal circuits of the cortex.

Conditioned-reflex memory of a food object should depend primarily on the structural development of synaptic mechanisms, in connection with the reverberation of excitation in the association neurons of forward and inverse temporary connections. In this process, complex structural changes in the region of the synaptic apparatus of temporary connections become apparent. Upon the formation of a conditioned-avoidance reflex in the corresponding motor area of the cortex, newly formed synaptic terminations, doubling and tripling of neuroglia, and doubling of the number of capillaries are observed. These changes should reinforce and prolong the reverberation of excitation in the later stages of increased excitability, and the reverberation of excitation, in turn, should facilitate the formation of active protein in the postsynaptic regions, which determine the plastic changes of the postsynaptic membrane. The more frequent the reinforcement of the conditional stimulus by the unconditional, i.e., by the food object, the more significant and longer the retention of these changes.

All these forms of memory—image, emotional, and conditioned-reflex—are a feature of all species of vertebrate animals. They gradually develop phylogenetically from fish to monkeys. These forms of memory are a feature of man as well, but adult man also has a special memory that is specific to him, i.e., verbal–logical memory.

The theoretical considerations set forth in this monograph as to the origin of different forms of memory are, to a considerable extent, working hypotheses that may serve as a point of departure for further investigation of this extremely complicated problem.

A deeper insight which is bound to be gained into the mechanisms of brain activity, especially with use of more thorough methods, will naturally yield new evidence on the molecular chemistry and ultrastructure of neural and glial elements, as well as on the physiological peculiarities and interconnections of cortical neurons. These new data will shed clearer light on the origin of the various forms of memory: image, emotional, and conditioned-reflex memory, and thus enable scientific understanding of the origin of the highest form of human memory—verbal–logical memory.

References

Adrianov O. S., and Mering T. A. (1959). *The Atlas of the Dog's Brain*, Moscow.

Aivazashvili, I. M. (1963). Emergence of images of food location and elaboration of automatized alimentary behavior in satiated dogs. *Bull. Acad. Sci. Georgian SSR* **30**: 59.

Aivazashvili, I. M. (1969). Dog's behavior following bilateral lesion of g. proreus. *Bull. Acad. Sci. Georgian SSR* (in press).

Aivazashvili, I. M., and Partskhaladze, N. N. (1968). A study of memory in dogs in ontogeny. *Bull. Acad. Sci. Georgian SSR* **50**: 481–486.

Akhmeteli, M. N. (1941). A study of imitation in pigeons. *Trans. Beritashvili Inst. Physiol.*

Albe Fessard, D., Rocha Miranda, C., and Oswaldo Cruz, F. (1960). Activités évoquées dans le noyau caudé du chat en réponse à des types divers d'afferences. *Electroencephalog. Clin. Neurophysiol.* **12**: 649–661.

Alikishibekova, Z. M. (1964). Secondary responses in the orbital cortex. *Bull. Acad. Sci. Azerb. SSR* **3**: 121.

Alikishibekova, Z. M. (1965). Spontaneous electrical activity, recruiting response, and primary response in the orbital cortex when the tongue and the lingual nerve are stimulated. In *The Problems of Visceral Reception of Physiologically Active Substances*, Acad. Sci. Azerb., SSR, Baku.

Auer, J. (1956). Terminal degeneration in the diencephalon after ablation of frontal cortex in the cat. *J. Anat.* **90**: 30–41.

Babich, F., Jacobson, A. L., Bubash, S., and Jacobson, A. (1965). Transfer of a response to naive rats by injection of ribonucleic acid extracted from trained rats. *Science* **149** (3684): 656.

Barondes, S. H. (1965). Relationship of biological regulatory mechanisms to learning and memory. *Nature*, **205**: 18–21.

Batting, K., and Rosvold, H. E. (1963). Psychophysiologische Leistungsfähigkeit des Macacus-Affen nach Cortexauschaltungen. *Ergeb. Physiol. biol. Chem. exptl. Pharmakol.* **52**: 157–204.

Beburishvili, N. A. (1937). Über die Einwirkung der Optischen und Akustischen Reizungen auf die Bewegungsreaktion beim Frosche. *Trans. Beritashvili Inst. Physiol.* **3**: 345.

Beburishvili, N. A., and Chichinadze, N. M. (1936). On the formation of individual behavior in frogs. *Trans. Tbilisi State Univ.* **2**: 127.

Bekaya, G. L. (1965). The change of electrical activity of the sensorimotor cortex during stimulation of the cerebellar tactile area. In *Current Problems of the Activity and Structure of Central Nervous System*, Metsniereba Press, Tbilisi, pp. 101–106.

Bekaya, G. L., and Moniava, E. S. (1963a). Projection of the cerebellum to the paleocortex. *Trans. Inst. Physiol. Georgian Acad. Sci.* **13**: 84.

Bekaya, G. L. and Moniava, E. S. (1963b). Some pathways connecting the cerebellum with the neocortex. *Trans. Inst. Physiol. Georgian Acad. Sci.*, **13**: 95.

Belenkov, N. U. (1965). *Conditioned Reflexes and Subcortical Structures of the Brain*, Meditsina, Moscow.

Beritashvili, I. S. (Beritoff, J.) (1925). Über die sukzessiven individuellen Reflexe. *J. Psychol. u. Neurol.* **32**: 29–56.

Beritashvili, I. S. (Beritoff, J.) (1927). Über die individuell-erworbene Tätigkeit des Zentralnervensystems. *J. Psychol. u. Neurol.*, **33**: 113–335.

Beritashvili, I. S. (1929). A comparative study of behavior in higher vertebrate animals. *Comm. I. Bull. Tbilisi Univ.* **10**: 15.

Beritashvili, I. S. (Beritoff, J. S.) (1932). *Individually-Acquired Activity of Central Nervous System*, Tbilisi.

Beritashvili, I. S. (Beritoff, J. S.) (1939). A comparative study of individual behavior in higher vertebrate animals. *Bull. Acad. Sci. USSR* **10**: 84.

Beritashvili, I. S. (Beritoff, J. S.) (1955). The change in an organism due to the effect of a concussion due to an explosion (observations on man and animals). *Trans. Inst. Physiol. Georgian Acad. Sci.* **6**: 1.

Beritashvili, I. S. (1959). *On Neural Mechanisms of Spatial Orientation in Higher Vertebrate Animals*, Tbilisi.

Beritashvili, I. S. (Beritoff, J. S.) (1960). The role of the cerebellum in spatial orientation of higher vertebrates. *Bull. Acad. Sci. USSR, S. biol.* **N4**: 481.

Beritashvili, I. S. (1961). The role of emotional excitation in behavior of higher vertebrates. *Trans. Inst. Physiol. Georgian Acad. Sci.* **12**: 17.

Beritashvili, I. S. (1963). The role of different brain areas in behavior of higher vertebrates, *Trans. Inst. Physiol. Georgian Acad. Sci.* **13**: 3.

Beritashvili, I. S. (Beritoff, J. S.) (1965). *Neural Mechanisms of Higher Vertebrate Behavior*, Translated and Edited by W. T. Liberson, Little, Brown and Co., Boston.

Beritashvili, I. S., and Aivazashvili, I. M. (1967). A study of memory in dogs during complex perception of the food location. *Sechenov Physiol. J. USSR* **53**: 236–243.

Beritashvili, I. S., and Aivazashvili, I. M. (1968). Duration of short-term memory in dogs in different experimental situations. In *Current Problems of the Activity and Structure of Central Nervous System*, Metsniereba Press, Tbilisi, pp. 29–44.

Beritashvili, I. S., and Dzidzishvili, N. N. (1934). A study of behavior in the microcephalus. *Trans. Biol. Section Transcaucasian Branch Acad. Sci. USSR* **2**:

Beritashvili, I. S., and Tsereteli, M. (1934). A study of individual behavior in dogs. *Sechenov Physiol. J. USSR* **17**: 184–195, 698–706.

Beritashvili, I. S., Aivazashvili, I. M., and Ordzhonikdze, Ts. A. (1965). Characteristics and origin of delayed reactions in dogs. In *Current Problems of the Activity and Structure of Central Nervous System*, Metsniereba Press, Tbilisi, p. 23.

Beritashvili, I. S. (Beritoff, J. S.), Bakuradze, A. N., and Katz, A. I. (1969). A study of image memory in primates. *Bull. Acad. Sci. Georgian SSR* (in press).

Bianki, V. L. (1967). *Evolution of Joint Function of the Cerebral Hemispheres*. Leningrad Univ. Press.

Bickford, R. G., Mulder, D. W., and Dodge, H. W., Jr., Svien, H. J., and Rome, H. P. (1958). Changes in memory function produced by electrical stimulation of the temporal lobe in man. *In* The Brain and Human Behavior, *Res. Publ. Assoc. Nerv. Ment. Dis.* **36**: 227.

Breathrach, A. S., and Goldby, F. (1954). The amygdaloid nuclei, hippocampus, and other parts of the rhinoencephalon in the porpoise (*Phocaena phocaena*). *J. Anat.* **88**: 267.

Bregadze, A. N. (1929). Contribution of comparative physiology of animal behavior. Formation of individual alimentary reflex in rabbits. *Bull. Tbilisi Univ.* **10**: 233.

Bregadze, A. N. (1945). Effect of cerebral contusion on individual behavior of animals due to an explosion. *Trans. Beritashvili Inst. Physiol.* **6**: 157–171.

Bregadze, A. N. (1948). Effect of emotional excitation on individual food behavior in dogs. *Abstracts of the First Transcaucasian. Dongr. Physiol. Biochem. Pharmacol.* p. 28.

Bregadze, A. N. (1950). Behavior of cats after removal of temporal lobes. *Trans. Beritashvili Inst. Physiol.* **8**: 241.

Bregadze, A. N., and Akhmeteli, M. N. (1969). Conditioned reflexes in kittens. *Trans. Tbilisi State Univ.* (in press).

Bregadze, A. N., Maisuradze, M. A., and Loria, Z. (1969). Study of memory in ontogeny. *Bull. Acad. Sci. Georgian SSR* (in press).

Bremer, F. and Stouple, N., "Facilitation et inhibition des potentiels évoqués corticaux dans l'éveil cérébral. *Arch. Intern. Physiol.* **67**: 240.

Brodal, A. (1957). *The Reticular Formation of the Brain Stem*, Oliver and Boyd, London.

Brutkowski, S. O. (1966). Functional peculiarities of the nonmotor frontal cortex in animals. In *The Frontal Lobes and Regulation of Psychic Processes*, pp. 100–115.

Brutkowski, S., Mishkin, M., and Rosvold, H. E. (1960). The effect of orbital and dorso-lateral frontal lesions on conditioned inhibitory reflexes in monkeys. *Acta Physiol. Polon.* **11**: 664–666.

Bures, J., Buresova, O., Weiss, T., Fifkova, E., and Bohdanecky, Z. (1962). Experimental study of the role of the hippocampus in conditioning and memory functions. In *Physiologie de l'Hippocampe*, Paris, pp. 241–257.

Buresova, O., and Bures, J. (1963). Physiology of recent memory. *Vopr. Psikhologii* **N6**: 63–74.

Buser, P., and Borenstein, P. (1959) Réponses somesthésiques, visuelles, et auditives, recueillies au niveau du cortex "associatif" suprasylvien chez le chat curarisé non anesthésié. *Electroencephalog. Clin. Neurophysiol.* **11**: 285–304.

Buser, P., Borenstein, P., and Bruner, J. (1959). Etude des systems "associatifs" visuels et auditifs chez le chat anesthésié au chloralose. *Electroencephalog. Clin. Neurophysiol.* **11**: 305–324.

Butkhuzi, S. M. (1962). Influence of the cerebral cortex on nucleus caudatus. *Bull. Acad. Sci. Georgian SSR.* **28**: 363–368.

Butkhuzi, S. M. (1963). On correlation of changes of the electroencephalogram and general motor activity of normal cats during stimulation of nucleus caudatus. *Trans. Inst. Physiol. Georgian Acad. Sci.* **13**: 61–68.

Butkhuzi, S. M. (1965). On the change of cortical evoked potentials during stimulation of caudate nucleus. In *Current Problems of the Activity and Structure of the Central Nervous System*, Metsniereba Press, Tbilisi, pp. 89–99.

Butkhuzi, S. M. (1965). Electrophysiological analysis of the cortical control of the nucleus caudatus. *Sechenov Physiol. J. USSR* **51**: 47–53.

Chichinadze, N. M. (1969). A study of psychonervous memory in mammals. *Trans. Tbilisi State Univ.* (in press).

Chorazyna, H., and Stepien, L. (1961). Impairment of recent auditory memory produced by cortical lesions in dog. *Acta Biol. Exp.* **21**: 177–187.

Crawford, M. P., Fulton, J. F., Jacobsen, C. F., and Wolfe, I. B. (1948). Frontal lobe ablation in Chimpanzee. In *The Frontal Lobe*, New York, pp. 3–58.

Delgado, M. R., Rosvold, H. E., and Looney, E. (1956). Conditional fear evoked by elec-trical stimulation of subcortical structures in the brain of monkeys. *J. Comp. Physiol. Psychol.* **49**: 373–380.

D'yachkova, L. N. (1964). Variations in the ultrastructure of synapses of the cerebral cortex in apes subjected to stimulation. *Dokl. Akad. Nauk SSSR* **155**: 227–229.

D'yachkova, L. N., Hamori, I., and Fedina, L., The ultrastructure of synapses in ganglion cliare of birds during ortho- and antidromic electric stimulation. *Dokl. Akad. Nauk SSSR* **172**: 957–959.

D'yachkova ,L. N., and Manteifel, U. B. (1969). Change in the ultrastructure of neurons of the midbrain tegmentum in frogs during excitation, *Arch. Anat. Histol. Embryol.* (in press).

Diebschlag, E. (1934). *Z. verlag. Physiol.* **21**: 343(N3).

Diebschlag, E. (1938). *Zool. Anz.* **124**: 30 (N1).

Dobrovolskii, V. (1911). On Alimentary Trace Reflexes. Dissertation.

Dumont, S. and Dell, P. (1958). Facilitation spécifiques et nonspécifiques des réponses visuelles corticales. *J. Physiol.* (Paris) **50**: 261.

Dzidzishvili, N. N. (1948). Receptor function of the skin. *Transc. Inst. Physiol. Georgian Acad. Sci.* **7**: 241–314.

Dzidzishvili, N. N. (1965). Pain reception. *J. Higher Nerv. Activ.* **15**: 1026–1035.

Dzidzishvili, N. N., and Butkhuzi, S. M. (1963). A study of the interaction of the cerebral cortex and the mesencephalic reticular formation in locomotor function. *Trans. Inst. Physiol Georgian Acad. Sci.* **13**: 69–76.

Dzidzishvili, N. N., and Ungiadze, A. A. (1969). Personal communication.

Eccles, J. C. (1961). The effects of use and disuse on synaptic function. In *Brain Mechanisms and Learning*, Oxford, pp. 335–358.

Eccles, J. C. (1964). The physiology of synapses. Academic Press, New York, p. 239.

Edds, M. V., Jr. (1953). *Quart. Rev. Biol.*, **28**: 260; Quoted by S. H. Barondes (1965). *Nature* **205**, No. 4966.

El'Darov A. L., and Sikharulidze, N. I. (1968). A study of the behavior of the turtle (*Emys orbicularis* and *Clemmys caspica*). *Dokl. Akad. nauk SSSR*, **182**: 237–239.

Eristavi, N. G. (1969). Electrical responses in the proreal gyrus evoked by peripheral stimulation. *Bull. Acad. Sci. Georgian SSR* (in press).

Frolov, U. P. (1926). Differentiation of conditioned stimuli in fish. *Russk. Physiol. Zh.* **9**: 113.

Flynn, J. P., MacLean, P. D., and Chul Kim (1961). Effects of hippocampal afterdischarges on conditioned responses. In D. E. Sheer (ed.), *Electrical Stimulation of the Brain*, University of Texas, p. 380–386.

Fujimoto, S. (1966). The fine structure of sympathetic ganglionic neuron of toad. In *Electron Microscopy*, Vol. 2. VI International Congress of Electron Microscopy, Tokyo, pp. 445–446.

Fulton, J. F. (1943). *Physiology of the Nervous System*, Oxford Univ. Press, pp. 418–428.

Fuster, J. M. (1957). Tachistoscopic perception in monkeys. *Federation Proc.* **16**: 43.

Fuster, J. M. (1958). Effect of stimulation of brain stem on tachistoscopic perception. *Science* **127**: 150.

Fuster, J. M., and Uyeda, A. A. (1962). Facilitation of tachistoscopic performance by stimulation of midbrain tegmental points in the monkey. *Exp. Neurol.* **6**: 384.

Galambos, R., and Morgan, C. T. (1956). The neural basis of learning. In *Handbook of Physiology. S. I. Neurophysiology*, Vol. 3, pp. 1471–1499.

Gastaut, H., and Hunter, J. (1950). An experimental study of the mechanism of photic activity in idiopathic epilepsy. *Electroenceph. Clin. Neurophysiol.* **2**: 263–287.

Gelashvili, N. A. (1968). Effect of X-radiation on delayed responses of rabbits. In *Current Problems of the Activity and Structure of the Central Nervous System*, Metsniereba Press, Tbilisi, pp. 45–67.

Gerard, R. W. (1961). The fixation of experience. In *Brain Mechanisms and Learning*, Oxford, pp. 21–36.

Glees, P., and Griffith, H. B. (1952). Bilateral destruction of the hippocampus (cornu ammonis) in a case of dementia," *Mschr. Psychiat. Neurol.* **123**: 193.

Glees, P. (1944). The anatomical basis of corticostriate connections. *J. Anat.* **78**: 47–51.

Goldberg, I. M., Diamond, J. T., and Neff, W. D. (1951). Auditory discrimination after ablation of temporal and insular cortex in cat. Federation Proc. **16**: 47.

Goldberg, J. M., Diamond, J. T., and Neff, W. D. (1958). Frequency discrimination after ablation of cortical projection areas of the auditory system. *Federation Proc.*, **17**: 55.

Gragg, B. (1965). Afferent connections of allocortex, *J. Anat.*, **99**: 339–357.

Grastyan, E. (1961). The significance of the earliest manifestations of conditioning in the mechanisms of learning. In *Brain Mechanisms and Learning*, Oxford, pp. 243–261.

Grastyan, E., and Karmos, G. (1962). Influence of hippocampal lesions in simple and delayed instrumental conditioned reflexes. In *Physiologie de l'Hippocampe*, Paris, pp. 225–239.

Grastyan, E., Lissak, K., Szabo, J., and Vereby, G. (1956). Über die funktionnelle Bedeutung des Hippocampus. In *Problems of Modern Physiology of Nervous and Muscle Systems*, Selected papers, dedic. I. S. Beritashvili, Tbilisi, pp. 67–80.

Gray, E. G. (1959). Axosomatic and axodendritic synapses of the cerebral cortex: an electron microscope study. *J. Anat.* **93**: 420–438.

Grossman, F. (1910). *Physiology of Trace Reflexes*, Dissertation.

Haggar, R. A., and Barr, M. L. (1950). Quantitative data on the size of synaptic end-bulbs in the cat's spinal cord," *J. Comp. Neurol.* **93**: 17.

Hebb, D. C. (1954). The problem of consciousness and introspection. In *Brain Mechanisms and Consciousness*, Oxford, pp. 402–421.

Hebb, D. C. (1961). Distinctive features of learning in the higher animal. In *Brain Mechanisms and Learning*, Oxford, pp. 37–53.

Hunter, W. S. (1913). The delayed reaction in animals' and childrens' behavior. *Comp. Psych. Monog.* **2** (N6): 86.

Hydén, H. (1965). Activation of nuclear RNA of neuron and glia in learning. *In* D. B. Kimble (ed.) *The Anatomy of Memory*, eliminate italics after memory *Proceedings of the First Conference on Learning, Remembering and Forgetting* pp. 172–239.

Hydén, H. (1960). The neuron. *In* J. Brachet and A. E. Mirsky (eds.) *The Cell*, Vol. 4. Academic Press, New York—London, pp. 215–323.

Hydén, H. (1964). The satellite cells in the nervous system. In *The Structure and Function of the Cell*, Selected papers, Moscow.

Isaacson, R. L., Douglas, R. J., and Moore, R. Y. (1960). The effect of radical hippocampal ablation on acquisition of avoidance response. *Amer. Psychol.* **15**: 486; (1961). *J. Comp. Physiol. Psychol.* **54**: 625.

Jacobsen, C. F. (1935). Experimental analysis of the functions of the frontal association areas in primates. *Arch. Neurol. Psychiat.* **34**: 884.

Jacobsen, C. F. (1935). Functions of the frontal association area in primates. *Arch. Neurol. Psychiat.* **33**: 558–569.

Jacobson, A. L., Babich, F. R., Bubash, S., and Jacobson, A. (1965). Differential-approach tendencies produced by injection of RNA from trained rats. *Science* **150** (No. 3696): 636.

Kaada, B. R. (1951). *Somatomotor Automatic and Electrographic Responses to Electrical Stimulation*, Oslo.

Kaada, B. R., Rasmussen, E. W., and Kveim, O. (1961). Effects of hippocampal lesions on maze learning and retention in rats. *Expl. Neurol.* **3**: 355.

Kadzhaya D. V. (1962). On the role of the cerebral hemispheres in the individually acquired behavior of chickens. *Bull. Acad. Sci. Georgian SSR* **29**: 459–464.

Kadzhaya D. (1970). On the study of memory in decorticated chickens. *Bull. Acad. Sci. Georgian SSR* (in press).

Karamian, A. I. (1956). *Functional Evolution of the Cerebellum and the Cerebral Hemispheres*, Moscow–Leningrad.

Kedia, I. A. (1969). Effect of lesion in the mesencephalic reticular formation on delayed reactions in cats. *Bull. Acad. Sci. Georgian SSR* (in press).

Kempinsky, W. H. (1951). Cortical projection of vestibular and facial nerves in cat. *J. Neurophysiol.* **14**: 203–210.

Khananashvili, M. M. (1961). Operation for the exclusion of function of the cerebral hemispheres. *Sechenov Physiol. J. USSR* **47**: 661–662.

Kholodov, U. A. (1963). Role of the main regions of the brain in fish while elaborating electrodefensive conditioned reflexes to different stimuli. In *The Neural Mechanisms of Conditioned Reflex Activity*, Moscow, pp. 287–296.

Kiknadze, G. I. (1968). Efferent cortical connections of the dog's propreal gyrus. *Bull. Acad. Sci. Georgian SSR* **51**: 775–778.

Kiknadze, G. I., and Mikeladze, A. L. (1968). Structural arrangement of the proreal gyrus. In *Current Problems of the Activity and Structure of the Central Nervous System*, Metsniereba Press, Tbilisi, pp. 291–300.

Klosovski, B. N., and Volzhina, N. S. (1956). On structural role of the caudate bodies. *Probl. Neurosurg. (USSR)* **1**: 8–14.

Kohler, W. (1921). *Intelligenzprüfung an Menschenaffen*, Berlin.

Kohler, W. (1929). *Gestalt Psychology*, New York.

Kometiani, P. A., and Aleksidze, N. G. (1967). *On Biochemical Mechanisms of Memory*. Tbilisi (in Georgian).

Konorski, J. (1959). A new method of physiological investigation of recent memory in animals. *Bull. de l'Akad. Polonaise des Sci.* Vol. 7, Chapter VI, pp. 115–117.

Konorski, J. (1960). Delayed responses or trace-conditioned reflex? *Sechenov Physiol. J. USSR* **46**: 244–246.

Konorski, J. (1961). The physiological approach to the problem of recent memory. In *Brain Mechanisms and Learning*, Oxford, pp. 115–132.

Konorski, J., and Lawicka, W. (1959). Physiological mechanisms of delayed reactions. The analysis and classification of delayed reactions," *Acta Biol. Exp.* **19**: 175–197.

Kostyuk, P. G. (1960). On the plasticity of synaptic connections," In *The Gagra Symposium*, Vol. 3, Tbilisi, p. 83.

Kruger, L. (1965). Morphological alteration of the cerebral cortex and its possible role in the loss and acquisition of information. *In* D. P. Kimble (ed.) *Proceedings of the First Conference on Learning, Remembering and Forgetting*, pp. 88–139.

Kuparadze, M. R. (1965). Plastic properties of the axons in the brain. In *Current Problems of the Activity and Structure of the Central Nervous System*, Metsniereba Press, Tbilisi, p. 213.

Kuparadze, M. R., and Kostenko, N. A. (1968). Cytochemical reactions of pyramidal cells of the dog's cerebral cortex during training. In *Proceedings of the Symposium on Reactive and Regenerative Processes in the Nervous System*, Tbilisi.

Kuypers, H. G. J. M. (1965). Szwarcbart, M. K., Mishkin, M., and Rosvold, H. E., Occipitotemporal corticocortical connections in the Rhesus monkey," *Exp. Neurol.*, **11**: 245–262.

Kvirtskhaliya, A. (1967). Emotions in cats without the neocortex. *Abstracts of Communications, Science Conference of the Biology Department*, Tbilisi Univ. Press.

Kvirtskhaliya, A. (1969). The role of olfactory perception of food in memory. *Abstracts of Communications. XIII Science Conference of Postgraduates and Young Science Workers*, Tbilisi Univ. Press.

Lashley, K. S. (1950). In search of the engram. *Symposium of Society for Experimental Biology*, IV, Cambridge, pp. 454–482.

Laursen, A. M. (1963). Corpus striatum. *Acta Physiol. Scand.* **59**, 211 (Suppl.).

Lawicka, W. (1957). Physiological analysis of the disturbances of the delayed reactions in dogs after prefrontal ablation. *Bull. de l'Akad. Polonaise des Sciences*. Vol. 5, Ch. VI, pp. 107–110.

Lawicka, W. (1958). Physiological mechanisms of delayed reactions. II. Delayed reaction in dogs and cats to directional stimuli. *Acta Biol. Exp.* **19**: 149–219.

Lawicka, W., and Konorski, J. (1959). Physiological mechanisms of delayed reaction. III. The effects of prefrontal ablation on delayed reactions in dogs. *Acta Biol. Exp.*, **19**: 221–231.

Leonov, W. (1926). Über die Bildung von bedingten Spurenreflexe bei Kindern. *Pflügers Arch.*, **214**: 304.

Leutskii, K. M. (1929). Conditioned reflexes in normal frogs and after removal of cerebral hemispheres. *Russk. Physiol. Zh.* **12**: 235.

Lindsley, D. B., Schreiner, L. H., Knowles, W. B., and Magoun, H. W. (1950). Behavioral and EEG changes following chronic brain stem lesions in the cat. *Electroencephalog. Clin. Neurophysiol.* **2**: 483–498.

Lissak, K., and Grastyan, E. (1957). The significance of activating systems and the hippocampus in the conditioned reflex. *Premier Congrès International des Sciences Neurologiques*, Bruxelles.

McCleary, R., and Moore, R. Y. (1965). *Subcortical Mechanisms of Behavior*, New York–London.

MacLean, P. D. (1957). Chemical and electrical stimulation of hippocampus in unrestrained animals. *Arch. Neurol. Psychiat.* **78**: 128.

Magoun, H. W. (1958). *The Waking Brain*, Springfield, Illinois.

Maisuradze M. (1970). On the study of amphibian behavior. *Bull. Acad. Sci. Georgian SSR* (in press).

Malyukina, G. A. (1955). Material for the Physiology of Lateral-Line Analyzers in Fish. Abstract of Dissertation, Moscow.

Mandell, A. J., and Bach, L. M. N. (1952). Production of anxiety behavior and avoidance conditioning by stimulation of bulbar reticular formation. *Proc. Soc. Exp. Biol. Med.* **97**: 880–896.

Mickle, W. A., and Ades, H. W. (1954). Rostral projection pathway of the vestibular system. *Amer. J. Physiol.* **176**: 243–246.

Mikeladze, A. L., and Kiknadze, G. I. (1966). Study of efferent cortical connections of the frontal lobes in the cat. *Bull. Acad. Sci. Georgian SSR* **42**: 737–742.

Mikeladze, A. L., and Kiknadze, G. I. (1969). Some afferent cortical connections of the proreal gyrus. *The Rorsakov J. Neuropathol. a. Psychiat.* (in press).

Miller, N. E. (1965). Chemical coding of behavior in the brain. *Science* **148**: 328–338.

Milner, B. (1962). Les troubles de la mémoire accompagnant des lésions hippocampiques bilaterales. In *Physiologie de l'hippocampe*, Paris p. 257.

Mishkin, M. (1957). Effects of small frontal lesions on delayed alternation in monkeys. *J. Neurophysiol.* 20: 615–622.

Mishkin, M. (1964). Perseveration of central sets after frontal lesions in monkeys. *In* J. M. Warren and K. Akert (ed.), *The Frontal Granular Cortex and Behavior*, New York.

Mishkin, M., and Pribram, K. H. (1954). Visual discrimination performance following partial ablation of the temporal lobe. I. Ventral vs. lateral. *J. Comp. Physiol. Psychol.*

Morrell, F. (1961). Lasting changes in synaptic organization produced by continuous neuronal bombardment. In *Brain Mechanisms and Learning*, Oxford, pp. 375–391.

Moruzzi, G., and Magoun, H. W. (1949). Brain stem reticular formation and activation of the EEG. *Electroencephalog. Clin. Neurophysiol.* **1**: 455.

Nakao, H. (1959). Emotional behavior produced by hypothalamic stimulation. *Amer. J. Physiol.* **194**: 411–419.

Naneishvili, T. L. (1967). The role of amygdala and pyriform cortex in the regulation of behavior. Abstract of Disseration, Tbilisi.

Narikashvili, S. P. (1950). Electrical activity of the brain stem, cerebral cortex, and cerebellum in unanesthetized cats. *Trans. Inst. Physiol. Georgian Acad. Sci.* **8**: 135–187.

Narikashvili, S. P. (1953). Effect of stimulation of subcortical structures on electrical activity of the cerebral cortex. *Trans. Inst. Physiol. Georgian Acad. Sci.* **9**: 133–154.

Narikashvili, S. P. (1961). Cortical regulation of function of the brain reticular formations. *Adv. Modern Biol. USSR* **52**: 257.

Narikashvili, S. P. (1962). *Nonspecific Structure of the Brain and Receptive Function of the Cereval Hemispheres*, Georgian Acad. Sci. Press, Tbilisi.

Narikashvili, S. P., Butkhuzi, S. M., Kajaia, D. V., and Moniava, E. S. (1963). Some characteristics of the reticular facilitation of visual responses. *Transac. Inst. Physiol. Georgian Acad. Sci.* **13**: 15–33.

Narikashvili, S. P., Butkhuzi, S. M., and Moniava, E. S. (1965). The study of the synchronizing mechanism of the brain stem reticular formation. In *Current Problems of the Activity and Structure of the Central Nervous System*, Metsniereba Press, Tbilisi, pp. 39–65.

Narikashvili, S. P., Moniava, E. S., and Kajaia, D. V. (1960). Contribution to the mechanism of interaction of the analyzers. *Dokl. Akad. Nauk SSSR* **134**: 229.

Nathan, P. W., and Smith, M. C. (1950). Normal mentality associated with a maldeveloped "rhinoencephalon." *J. Neurol. Neurosurg. Psychiat.* **13**: 191.

134   References

Natishvili, T. A. (1969). A study of delayed reactions in dogs with intact and damaged labyrinths. *Bull. Acad. Sci. Georgian SSR* (in press).
Natishvili, T. A. (1968). Delayed reactions in experimental naive dogs. *Bull. Acad. Sci. Georgian SSR* **51**: 773–758.
Natishvili, T. A., and Sikharulidze, N. I. (1968). The role of the inferior and medial parts of the temporal lobe in a dog's behavior. *Bull. Acad. Sci. Georgian SSR* **49**: 725–730.
Nauta, W. J. H. (1960). Some neural pathways related to the limbic system. *In* E. R. Ramey and D. S. O'Doherty (eds.) *Electrical Studies on the Unanesthetized Brain*, Hoeber, pp. 1–16.
Nauta, W. J. H. (1964). Some efferent connections of the prefrontal cortex in the monkey. In *The Frontal Granular Cortex and Behavior*, New York, pp. 357–409.
Nutsubidze, M. A. (1961). The role of hippocampal gyrus in the emotional reactions of cats. *Bull. Acad. Sci. Georgian SSR* **26**: 79–86.
Nutsubidze, M. A. (1963). Emotional reactions in cats evoked by stimulation of the cingulate gyrus. *Trans. Inst. Physiol. Georgian Acad. Sci.* **13**: 103–113.
Nutsubidze, M. A., and Ordzhonikidze, Ts. A. (1961). On behavioral reactions of the cat after removal of the neocortex. *Trans. Inst. Physiol. Georgian Acad. Sci.* **12**: 85–93.
Obraztsova, G. A. (1964). *Problems of Ontogeny of Higher Nervous Activity*. Nauka, Moscow.
Obukhova, G. P. (1959). A study of the descending pathways of the occipital cortex (fields 17, 18, 19) to the subcortical structures. *Annual Trans. Inst. Exp. Med. Acad. Med. Sci. USSR* **5**.
Okudzhava, V. M. (1959). Posttetanic potentiation of dendritic potentials in the cerebral cortex. *Dokl. Akad. nauk SSSR* **128**: 635.
Oniani, T. N., and Ordzhonikidze, TsA. (1968). Changes in electrical activity of some brain structures of the cat during general behavioral reactions. In *Current Problems of the Activity and Structure of the Central Nervous System*, Metsniereba Press, Tbilisi, pp. 5–13.
Ordzhonikidze, Ts.A. (1963). Effect of lesion in the nucleus caudatus on the cat's behavior, *Trans. Inst. Physiol. Georgian Acad. Sci.* **13**: 113.
Odzhonikidze, Ts. A., and Nutsubidze, M. A. (1961). The role of the paleocortex in emotional reactions of the cat. *Trans. Inst. Physiol. Georgian Acad. Sci.* **12**: 95–106.
Patton, H. D., and Amassian, V. E. (1952). Cortical projection zone of the chorda tympani nerve in the cat, *J. Neurophysiol.* **15**: 245–250.
Penfield, W. (1954). Studies of the cerebral cortex of man. In *Brain Mechanisms and Consciousness*, Oxford, pp. 284–313.
Penfield, W., and Milner, B. (1958). Memory deficit produced by bilateral lesions in the hippocampal zone. *Arch. Neurol. Psychiat.* **79**: 475–487.
Polyakov, K. L. (1930). Physiology of olfactory and auditory analyzers in tortoise. *Russk. Physiol. Zh.* **13**: 161.
Popov, N. F. (1953). *Investigation into the Physiology of the Brain in Animals*, Moscow.
Pribram, K. H. (1950). Some physical and pharmacological factors affecting delayed response performance of baboons following frontal lobotomy. *J. Neurophysiol.* **13**: 373–382.
Pribram, K. (1964). Perspectives in the development of neuropsychology. *Vopr. Psychol.* **10** (N2): 16–26.
Pribram K. H., and Bagshaw M. H. (1953). Further analysis of the temporal lobe syndrome utilizing frontotemporal ablation. *J. Comp. Neurol.* **99**: 347–375.
Pribram, K. H., and Mishkin, M. (1955). Simultaneous and successive visual discrimination by monkeys with inferotemporal lesions. *J. Comp. Physiol. Psychol.* **48**: 198.
Purpura, D. P. (1961). Analysis of axodendritic synaptic organizations in an immature cerebral cortex. *Ann. N. Y. Acad. Sci.* **94**: 604–655.
Ramon y Cajal, S. (1959). *Degeneration and Regeneration of the Nervous System, Vol. 2*, Hafner Publishing Company, New York, pp. 656–676; (1961). *Ann. Rev. Physiol.* **26**: 560.

Rinvik, E. (1966). The corticonigral projection in the cat. *J. Comp. Neurol.* **126**: 241–255.

Roitbak, A. I. (1953). Oscillographic study of the foci of increased excitability in the cerebral hemispheres. *Trans. Inst. Physiol. Georgian Acad. Sci.* **9**: 97–131.

Roitbak, A. I. (1964). Origin and physiological significance of surface negative potentials in the cortex. *Abstracts of X Sci. Conference Inst. Physiol. Georgian Acad. Sci.*, pp. 46–48.

Roitbak, A. I. (1956). Metamorphosis of neural responses. In *Problems of Modern Physiology of Nervous and Muscular Systems*, Inst. Physiol. Georgian Acad. Sci., Tbilisi, p. 243.

Romanyuk, A. (1964). The formation of defensive conditioned reflexes by direct stimulation of the hypothalamus in a cat. *Acta Biol. Exp.* **24** (N3): 145–153.

Rosvold, H. E., and Mishkin, M. (1961). Nonsensory effects of frontal lesions on discrimination learning and performance. In J. F. Delafresnaye (ed.) *Brain Mechanisms and Learning*, Oxford, pp. 555–576.

Rosvold, H. E., Szwarcbart, M. E. (1964). Neural structure involved in delayed response performance. In J. M. Warren and K. Akert (ed.) *The Frontal Granular Cortex and Behavior*, New York, pp. 1–15.

Ruwaldt, M. M., and Snider, R. S. (1956). Projections of vestibular areas of the cerebellum to the cerebrum. *J. Comp. Neurol.* **104**: 387–401.

Schmitt, F. (1962). Psychophysics on molecular levels. In M. Kasha and B. Pullman (eds.) *Horizons in Biochemistry*, Albert Szent-Györgyi Dedicatory Volume, Academic Press, New York, London.

Scoville, W. B., and Milner, B. (1957). Loss of recent memory after bilateral hippocampal lesions. *J. Neurol. Neurosurg. Psychiat.* **20**: 11.

Serkov, F. N., and Palamarchuk, I. G. (1960). Changes in electrical activity of the cortex and of some subcortical structures during alimentary and defense reflexes. *Gagra Symposium* **3**: 363–371.

Sharpless, S. K. (1964). Reorganization of function in the nervous system use and disuse. *Ann. Rev. Physiol.* **26**: 257–388.

Shkolnik-Yarros, E. G. (1958). A study of the efferent pathways of the visual cortex. *J. Higher Nerv. Activ.* **8**: 123–136.

Shustin, N. A. (1953). Trace-conditioned reflex in dogs following removal of the frontal lobes. *Trans. Pavlov Inst. Physiol.* **2**: 72–85.

Shustin, N. A. (1959). *Physiology of the Cerebral Frontal Lobes*, Medgiz.

Sikharulidze, N. I. (1962). Some data obtained with partial and complete removal of the visual analyzer in dogs. *Bull. Acad. Sci. Georgian SSR* **28**: 355.

Sikharulidze, N. I. (1966). A study of behavior in reptiles (Tortoise). *Bull. Acad. Sci. Georgian SSR* **43**: 3.

Sikharulidze, N. I. (1967). A study of individually-acquired behavior in fish. *Bull. Acad. Sci. Georgian SSR* **45**: 3.

Sikharulidze, N. I. (1969). A study of individually-acquired behavior in lizards. *Trans. Tbilisi State Univ.* (in press).

Sikharulidze, N. I. (1969). The role of the telencephalon in behavior of fish. *Dokl. Akad. nauk SSSR* **153**: 193–196.

Sikharulidze, N., and Kadagishvili, A. (1969). The role of the forebrain and cerebellum in the behavior of lizards. *Bull. Acad. Sci. Georgian SSR* (in press).

Skrebitskii, V. G., and Shkolnik-Yarros, E. G. (1964). A study of the visual representation in the cerebral cortex. *J. Higher Nerv. Activ.* **14**: 276–286.

Smirnov, G. D. (1967). Ultrastructure of synapses and the problem of synaptic transmission. *Adv. Modern Biol.* **63**: 247–260.

Smirnov, G. D. (1968). Functional arrangement of neural centers. *Bull. Acad. Sci. USSR* **N1**: 48–59.

Sokolov, E. N. (1960). Neuronal models and the orienting reflex. In M. A. D. Brazier (ed.) *The Central Nervous System and Behavior*, New York, pp. 187–276.

Sprague, J. M., Chambers, W. W., and Stellar, E. (1961). Attentive, affective, and adaptive behavior in the Cat. *Science* **133**: 33–41.

Sprague, J. M., Levitt, M., Robson, K., Liu, C. N., Stellar, E., and Chambers, W. W. (1963). A neuroanatomical and behavioral analysis of the syndromes resulting from midbrain lemniscal and reticular lesions in the cat. *Arch. Ital. Biol.* **101**: 225–296.

Starzl, T. E., and Whitlock, D. G. (1952). Diffuse thalamic projection system in a monkey. *J. Neurophysiol.*, **15**: 449.

Stratford, J. (1954). Corticothalamic connections from gyrus proreus and the first and second somatic sensory areas of the cat. *J. Comp. Neurol.* **100**: 1–14.

Ten Cate, J. (1934). Akustische und optische Reaktionen der Katzen nach teilweisen und totalen Extirpationen des Neopalliums. *Arch. Neerland. Physiol.* **19**: 191–264.

Tevzadze, V. (1968). Effect of hippocampal direct stimulation on reflex reaction of animals. In *Current Problems of the Activity and Structure of the Central Nervous System*, Metsniereba Press, Tbilisi, pp. 86–96.

Topurya, Sh. R. (1926). Elaboration and differentiation of conditioned defense reflexes in puppies. *Bull. Tbilisi State Univ.* **10**: 253.

Tsintsadze, D. G. (1968). A study of the role of the lemniscal system in behavior of cats. *Bull. Acad. Sci. Georgian SSR* **49**: 237–242.

Tskipuridze, L. R., and Bakuradze, A. N. (1948). Interrelation between slow bioelectric potentials in the cerebral cortex and those in the cerebellar cortex. *Trans. Inst. Physiol. Georgian Acad. Sci.* **8**: 201–214.

Vastola, E. F. (1961). A direct pathway from the lateral geniculate body to the association cortex. *J. Neurophysiol.* **24**: 469–487.

Victor, M. (1964). Observations on the amnestic syndrome in man and its anatomical basis. In M. A. B. Brazier (ed.) *Brain Function, Calif. Univ. Press*, Berkeley, pp. 311–340.

Voitonis, N. (1940). Behavior of monkeys from the point of view of anthropogenesis. *Under the Standard of Marxism* N9: 130–145.

Wagner, H. (1933). *Z. Vergl. Physiol.* **18**: 378.

Warren, J. M. (1964). The behavior of carnivores and primates with lesions in the prefrontal cortex. In *The Frontal Granular Cortex and Behavior*, New York, pp. 188–191.

Webster, K. (1965). The corticostriatal projection in the cat. *J. Anat.* **99**: 329–337.

Weiskrantz, L., and Mishkin, M. (1958). Effects of temporal and frontal cortical lesions on auditory discrimination in monkeys. *Brain* **81**: 406–414.

Wilson, M. (1957). Effects of circumscribed cortical lesions upon somesthetic discrimination in the monkey. *J. Comp. Physiol. Psychol.* **50**: 630–635.

Wilson, W. A., Jr., and Mishkin, M. (1959). Comparison of the effects of inferotemporal and lateral occipital lesions on visually guided behavior in monkeys. *J. Comp. Physiol. Psychol.* **52**: 10–17.

Yoshii, N., Matsumoto, J., Ogura, H., Shimokochi, M., Yamagouchi, Y., and Yamasaki, H. (1960). Conditioned reflex and electroencephalography. In H. H. Jasper and G. D. Smirnov (eds.) *Moscow Colloquium on EEG of Higher Nervous Activity*, Montreal, pp. 199–211.

Zelenyi, G. P. (1911–1912). A dog after removal of the cerebral hemisphere," Comm. I and II, *Bull. Soc. Russian Physicians* **80**: (5): 471.

Zelenyi, G. P. (1930). Results of removal of the cerebral hemispheres. *Med. Biol. J.* **6**. (N1–2): 1.

Index